Author, bushman and raconteur Phil O'Brien,
heading off on another misadventure.

About the Author

Phil O'Brien spent his early years on a remote cattle station
in the Northern Territory. A severe drought brought him
and his family down to Adelaide when he was just a boy,
but security and the suburbs never really appealed to
him and when he was old enough to drive he blew out of
town and headed bush. Twenty-five years and about two
hundred jobs later, Phil's still out there, roaming from
job to job and place to place and meeting all sorts of
characters along the way.

Described by Westpac Bank as 'nomadic', he is a
financial disaster with no fixed address. But whichever
way you look at it, he's got some great stories to tell! And
in his own way, Phil has turned drifting around outback
Australia into an art form . . .

101
ADVENTURES
that got me absolutely nowhere

by PHIL O'BRIEN

A Campfire Singer Production
Box 257 Katherine 0850 Northern Territory
Australia

ISBN 978-0-9580667-1-6

Phil O'Brien can be contacted at campfiresinger@hotmail.com

Cover and internal designs by Christabella Designs
Typeset in 12/15pt Minion by Kirby Jones
Colour Reproduction by Graphic Print, SA
Printed and Bound in Australia by Griffin Press, Adelaide

I'd like to dedicate this book to the open road,
a good steak sandwich . . .
and the people you meet along the way.

Contents

Introduction

Just as the wind, rain, fire and heat have shaped this rugged landscape, life's experiences can shape a bloke and determine the way he is. On a good day we evolve, and on a bad day we can sometimes erode away a little bit.

Every day we are caressed by the winds of fate, and we sail the seas of change, and we become the person we are.

The washing machine of life chugs on relentlessly, and I personally have been maxi-washed, spun dry and spun out. I've also had a right royal rinsing and been hung out to dry on more than one occasion. But that's the washing machine of life for you — expect the unexpected.

As a kid I was lucky to have a dad who was a total optimist and he instilled that mindset into me at a young age. I was taught never to feel sorry for myself, no matter how tough the situation. Self-pity was never an option in my family and a bloke just had to dust himself off and try again.

My old man was a good cattleman and he was the son of a good cattleman, but after a ten-year drought in the harsh remoteness of Central Australia the dynasty was cut short. The family packed up and we headed down to

Phil, aged three, discussing cattle prices with his mum and dad, Glenda and Jack, at Tempe Downs Station, Northern Territory.

the southern city of Adelaide, to start a new life. At that stage I was just a young kid.

Well, they took the boy out of the bush but someone forgot to take the bush out of the boy, and after I finished my schooling, I knew in my heart it was time to go back and become what I was meant to be. So I unchained the shackles of society and I set myself free ... More than twenty years and about two hundred jobs later, the journey continues.

It's been an uncomplicated life, many miles travelled and many friends made. There have been a lot of good campfires and bad hangovers. At times I've lost my direction and run off the rails. There has been quiet lonely times, camped in the bush, staring into the coals for hours, wondering where life would take me next. But I always take each day as it comes and I keep trying, fuelled by the endless optimism that was my heritage.

Over the years, the one and only really consistent aspect of my life, the one thing I can totally rely on, has been the unreliability of my financial situation. My total package these days is an old Toyota, a guitar and a swag — not what you'd call real financial security. But when I'm out on the open road, thumping along in the old diesel, I feel like a king. I've tasted freedom . . . and that's got to be worth something.

But you try explaining that to a person who works at the bank. Sometimes I think I must have 'Big Risk' tattooed across my forehead. Friends made and memories stowed away will be my superannuation policy. A cold beer and pleasant thoughts of places and people, that'll be my retirement package.

Lady Luck dealt me an interesting card a while back and it was the best I've had in recent times. I was at a party getting well on the way to being half cut and telling

Phil, aged three, Tempe Downs Station, Northern Territory. Sitting on a cactus holding a chook was probably the first real adventure that got him absolutely nowhere.

yarns about the things I'd been doing over the years. There happened to be a professional writer there by the name of David Harris who found my stories interesting. He pulled me aside and pointed out that if I could somehow write these stories down, people might like to read them. Anyway, for a bloke like me this presented such a huge challenge I found I just had to have a crack.

So here we are, friends and lovers of fine literature, I took his advice. Writing this book has taken a fragmented life and given it direction, and I'll always be grateful to David Harris for that. I hope you enjoy these stories from my life, a life of complete misadventure. I've kept it raw and honest. So you'd better fasten your emotional seat belt and strap in for the journey, because it's gunna be a rough ride and the grammar's gunna get ugly. I sincerely hope *101 Adventures that got me absolutely nowhere* takes you to places you've never been before — I just hope you can handle it!

Old Morris

The Greyhound bus dropped me just outside the old bush pub, the nerve centre of a bustling town of about fifteen people. Although it wasn't the end of the world, if you shut your eyes you could sense it wasn't far away.

I was a young bloke who was going to take the bush by storm. You know what I mean — I was gunna ride everything, break in everything, castrate everything, dehorn everything ... and make love to anything. Adventure and romance, here we go!

I'd lined myself up a job on a cattle station, about 250 kilometres from nowhere, and the manager, a bloke that went by the name of Old Morris, was due to fly in and pick me up in his aeroplane about midday. I was a bit early, so I thought I'd give the local economy a boost and bang a few cold ones down while I waited.

As usual, one led to about six as I yarned to the barman and an old rabbit-trapper who'd wandered in. Looking back, I was glad I got the opportunity to have a few quick beers because I think it helped numb the senses a bit. Although I didn't realise it, a terrifying ordeal was just around the corner.

I soon heard the drone of an aircraft coming in, louder and louder, until it sounded like the plane had landed and taxied in right up to the back door of the pub — and I'll be buggered, it had! I grabbed my swag and headed out, and there he was, Old Morris.

He was standing in front of the plane completely motionless, like some kind of stone monument. His forearms were huge and they hung down around his waist as if he was about to draw a gun. His hat was a real ball-tearer and with the sun behind it, it cast a huge shadow out across the red dirt, giving the impression he was standing under some kind of rock overhang.

He must have been about seventy, I guessed. He just stared at me. He was built like a besser-block shithouse, still powerful for his age, sun-dried and tough. This bloke was 100 per cent country and he didn't come across as a chatty sort of guy. He sized me up, not looking real impressed. Then, out of the blue, he raised his arm and jerked his thumb back in the direction of the aircraft.

Now the plane looked like an old Toyota Corolla with wings, and when we climbed in Old Morris's hat took up two-thirds of the cabin space, not leaving me much room at all. He still hadn't spoken. I was starting to feel a little nervous as I hate flying at the best of times and Morris's rig wasn't a late-model job. It looked more like something he'd put together himself out in the back shed over a couple of Sundays.

He started clawing at the dash, then pulled something, then twisted something, and then really reefed on something, and the old girl fired. He gave it some herbs and we chugged off down the gravel strip, waves of red dust going everywhere. I was feeling extremely anxious about the whole turnout and thoughts of Buddy Holly's air disaster came drifting through my mind. Then Old Morris must have figured it was time to give her full throttle, because he nearly tore it clean out of the dash!

After a wild buck we pig-rooted off across the flat, Morris at the helm with a look on his face that said he was taking this baby to hell and back. Somehow we defied gravity and Old Morris had her going straight up. I mean that literally — it wasn't a gradual ascent, we were just blasting straight up, Morris leaning back in the seat with his legs stretched out in front of him as if he was in the saddle, completely expressionless.

I looked out and noticed the rivets on the wing were rattling around loosely. This was no joke. Then Old Morris completely let go of the controls, leaned back, pulled out his tobacco and proceeded to roll himself a smoke. The plane was going all over the place, like one of those acrobatic planes at an air show doing loop-the-loops.

Morris finally finished building the cigarette and, as he hung it off his bottom lip, decided to grab the controls again and level out, which was a good move as we seemed to be going so far up we weren't far from launching straight into outer space. Every time I looked out the window, all I could see was the rivets rattling around on the wing and I was sure there weren't as many there as when we first started!

The smoke from Morris's rollie was now starting to engulf the cabin and it was getting hard to breathe. I shut my eyes, half-expecting us to blow up any minute and blaze through the sky like a comet. Next thing he starts clutching at his chest. Through the smoke-haze I see him pull a little transistor radio from his pocket. He pokes it at me and says, 'Get a score.' Old Morris was a man of few words, three to be exact.

I presumed he meant cricket score as I knew the Aussies were playing the Kiwis at the time, but no luck, it was all static.

So on we sailed and I was working myself up into a state of sheer uncontrollable terror. I was ready to shit volcanic rock.

Old Morris, going for the tobacco again, as calm as you like, and here we go again . . . no hands! Onwards we soared, the plane shooting all over the sky, Morris trying to get his lighter to work and finally, thank God, it did. Then out came the transistor again, Old Morris clamping it to his ear, and it sounded like he made contact.

The cricket score was priority number one, followed closely by the roll-your-own, then a bit further down the list was steering the plane.

The trip probably only took about an hour, but it felt like forever, it felt like I'd never been anywhere else but inside that plane shitting myself. But the station finally came into view and I nearly burst into tears from joy. It was the first time since we kicked off that I felt we might actually make it alive.

Morris sent her straight down like a dive-bomber. No gradual descent, he was taking the direct approach. Relentless, transistor clamped on his ear, smoke billowing from his gob, he just kept her going straight for the station's shiny tin roofs. I could feel the G-force contorting my face. Down we speared, me clawing at the armrest, feeling like I was just about to lose my lunch and the six cans of beer I'd slugged down before joining Old Morris's flying circus. A shed was coming up and I'm thinking, is he gunna make it? *Aaaaaaaaah!*

There wouldn't have been more than a cigarette paper in it as we skimmed over the corrugated iron roof. Morris, unfazed, banked hard left to avoid wearing a windmill, then on down to the airstrip, and as the wheels touched down the red dust exploded. Old Morris, the transistor radio, myself and the rivets rattled along the ground, rocks pinging everywhere as he taxied the old girl through a sea of dust up to the shed we'd nearly collected a few minutes ago.

He cut the engine and jerked a thumb in the direction of the door, so I climbed out and, fairly jelly-legged, ducked around the corner for an extremely well-deserved leak. When I came back I could see him heading for the homestead, tranny still fixed to one ear, casual as you like.

This trip did nothing to build my confidence in flying, but one thing's for sure, it felt great to still be alive! It's amazing how a near-death experience can really take it out of you. I was buggered. I got my gear together and hung around the plane for a minute, just letting my nerve endings untangle themselves. It wasn't long before Old Morris turned up again, this time with his wife.

She looked so very petite next to Morris, who still had the transistor jammed to his ear. Old Morris obviously didn't feel the need to actually speak but he looked at his wife then swung his gaze at me and I realised this was probably the official introduction. His facial expression was similar to that of a mud brick, totally non-committal.

His wife was very prim and proper, and I doubted she'd ever passed wind in her whole life. She wasn't actually wearing a hooped skirt and a lace bonnet, but she appeared to be from a by-gone era, extremely straitlaced. I couldn't work out how she'd ever tied up with a bloke like Morris, who was still doing his best impersonation of Ayers Rock.

Now Morris's wife was very polite but she let it be known that she liked things pretty shipshape. It was her way or the highway, and the highway was 270 kilometres away. I got the message: buckle down, work hard, get your seventy bucks a week and don't make any trouble.

With a hand signal Morris pointed out my accommodation — an old caravan parked up next to the shed — and they left me to settle in.

Up to about an hour and fifteen minutes ago, I'd had the equation all worked out. Banjo Paterson multiplied by the Man from Snowy River equalled me. But as I lay on my bunk staring up at the cobwebs in the caravan, reality started to flood in. There were no pubs in sight, no girls, no grog, no nothing. This was isolation in a hard part of the country, and I had to learn how to handle it. I was determined this was going to be a character-building experience and I was going to do the right thing and see it through. In a few months I could be the centrefold in the R. M. Williams mail-order catalogue. Not only would my manners be as impeccable as old Morris's wife had suggested, but in years to come I'd be remembered as one of the all-time great jackaroos of outback history.

A jackaroo, for those of you that aren't familiar with the term, is an apprentice stockman, a young bloke learning the ropes of stock and station work. Now the only thing on a Territory cattle station that's lower than a jackaroo is a new jackaroo. I realised this when the other two young jackaroos turned up at the caravan around sunset. They went into quite a bit of detail explaining this to me.

Apart from those two living legends, there was the head stockman, his wife and two Aboriginal blokes living on the station. There was the homestead where Morris and his wife lived, surrounded by neat lawns and a pack of crazed blue heeler dogs that doubled as pets. There were several sheds, some new, some old, and a set of cattle yards, a windmill and tanks. And across a dry creek bed a few hundred metres away there was another shed where the Aboriginal fellas lived.

The surrounding country was fairly flat with the odd rocky little hill and gum trees lining the creeks. In its own rugged way it was pretty scenic. Not long after I arrived the station received some big rains, which is most welcome in that country, and soon the red ochre of the landscape turned to green as the country transformed itself.

I'm not sure how hard the slaves worked in the cotton plantations of America back in the 1800s but it couldn't have been any harder than I worked in the weeks ahead. I think Old Morris and his wife were disappointed when the sun went down and the daylight ran out, otherwise they would have worked me right around the clock. I did mile after mile of fencing, yard-building, concreting, windmill maintenance, pick-and-shovel work and anything else that needed doing. I even dug a vegetable garden for Morris's wife while she stood there cracking the whip.

Sometimes me and the other two jackaroos would work together and other times we'd split up doing different things. It was always very competitive when we were together, as it often is with young blokes, and they were pretty keen to please Old Morris and his wife.

It all came unstuck for them one day when Morris's wife came around and wanted to know if anyone required a haircut. The two other jackaroos couldn't answer quick enough. 'Oh yeah, that would be great,' they said, trying to gain brownie points with Old Morris's wife. Trying to climb the social ladder on a Territory cattle station is pretty futile, but the boys were giving it their best shot.

So she came back with a chair and an old saucepan and she sat the first lad on the chair and we're wondering what she's going do with the saucepan. With a flick of the

Phil with friendly cow, Old Morris's cattle station.

wrist she jammed it on the bloke's head and cut around the edge with an old pair of scissors. It only took about three minutes and the job was done.

It was one of the wildest haircuts I'd ever seen and also one of the roundest. The other bloke had turned green with fear, just like someone next in line for the gallows. It took all my strength not to piss myself laughing. The two jackaroos were pretty devastated and went straight for their hats, but they still thanked her.

With the saucepan in one hand and the scissors in the other she came at me like the grim reaper, but I pulled her up by saying my old man always reckoned you should leave a bit of hair on the back of the neck because it helps in stopping sunstroke. So she spared me, but she wasn't happy about it.

Apart from Morris's wife's haircuts there were other dangers on the station, like the crazed pack of blue heelers that patrolled constantly. They took great delight in waiting till I went to the outside dunny about fifty metres from the caravan. I'd be in there doing the business and I could hear them heavy breathing just outside the corrugated iron door. I knew it was gunna be on. Eventually I'd work up the courage to make a run for it, but no matter how hard I came out of the blocks they'd be onto me and they'd really hook in.

For anyone interested in a track-and-field career this would have been good training, as you'd end up shaving quite a bit of time off your personal best. But getting mauled by a pack of dogs after a fourteen-hour day wasn't what I call fun. While Morris was around they didn't behave too bad — like everyone else on the station, they responded to his hand signals.

Old Morris fell off a windmill while I was there, but no one knew what had happened because he didn't talk about it. The fall would probably have killed anyone else but he survived it and came back with just a slight limp, which was the only time I'd seen him show emotion. His wife generally showed enough emotion for both of them. As the weeks went on she really ripped into me a few times — I don't think she ever got over the fact I wouldn't get a haircut. I'd say she took that one to the grave.

The country had turned very lush and green and was bursting with life. Cattle started putting on condition and mobs of brumbies started to turn up, instinctively following the rain and the good feed that followed. Waterhens congregated, the desert rose bloomed and frogs came from near and far. The frogs must have heard the surf was up in the old tin dunny because they moved in there by the hundreds, which made going to the toilet even more interesting.

Rain is the key in Central Australia and this was a particularly good year. The country was really responding. Old Morris responded as well — he decided it was a good time to muster his cattle and have a look at them, maybe sell a few off. This meant a lot of camping out and a lot of hours in the saddle. My fourteen-hour day increased to fourteen hours plus however long it took to get the job done.

Life got leaner and life got meaner, and for the next six or seven weeks I chased Morris's not-too-friendly cattle up rocky hill and down rocky dale. We lived on corned beef and damper and operated out of the swag, moving from one part of Morris's huge property to the other. While the mustering was going on Morris mainly stayed around the homestead, keeping things going there, but at certain times he'd come out to where we were camped and inspect his cattle.

These cattle weren't pets and they'd often turn on you. Believe me, it's no fun running around with a one-ton Brahman bull up your arse. But Old Morris showed absolutely no fear as he walked around a mob of freshly yarded cattle. Smoke balanced on his bottom lip, he'd stroll through the cattle and they'd part before him, just like the Red Sea for Moses. Sometimes you'd lose sight of him but you could see his hat moving in and out around the cattle, and you presumed he was still under it. He was fearless and he was tough and I think even the cattle sensed it.

Morris got us all together one day and with a few hand signals and the help of his wife passed on the good news that we were taking a break and going into town for the Easter Race weekend. I'd now done roughly three hard months on the place without a day off, without a beer and without any romantic interest at all. At the mere thought of a beer my tongue would swell and I'd nearly black out. The only woman I'd had anything to do with was Morris's wife and she wasn't the type you dream about while you're lying in your swag that's for sure.

My apprenticeship had been tough. I'd been bitten, kicked and stomped on by just about every horse on the place, worked into the ground, underpaid, underfed, threatened with a haircut from hell and interfered with by a mob of blue heelers. But I was still keen and determined to make a name for myself. I was a jackaroo with a future. Still, a few quiet cold beers over Easter sounded mighty good.

When the day came to head off I was chafing at the bit. After getting our pay cheques from Old Morris, we were treated to a lecture from his wife on appropriate behaviour in town. We were representing the station and were to act accordingly, like ambassadors. I could feel the cheque already heating up in my pocket, and I think it was starting to smoke.

Old Morris jerked a thumb in the direction of his rattly old aeroplane which meant he and his wife would be flying into town, so all us young blokes were to take the old Toyota and give the two Aboriginal blokes a ride in as well. Another wave of the hand and some bottom lip movement also signified that the head stockman and his wife would be taking their own vehicle in, and we were all to meet up at the camp-ground.

The little town was a 270-kilometre trip on a not-so-good dirt track. We all piled on the back, and with swags rolled we rattled off. The young jackaroo driving didn't seem real safety-conscious as he swung the wheel from left to right driving way too fast for the conditions. Sure enough, skidding around a corner we hit a big pothole and one bloke fell off the back onto the road, smashing up a few ribs and knocking the hell out of himself. We reversed up and put him back on the tray. He was in a lot of pain so we decided to make a slight detour and head for a small Aboriginal community where we knew there was a clinic. Luckily the Sister was there on duty but she didn't seem real interested. The treatment he got left a lot to be desired — two aspro with some Deep Heat for the ribs. I thought she could have done more, but he seemed happy enough.

Meanwhile, a crowd was forming around the Toyota. Everyone wanted a lift into town for the races. When we finally pulled out of the community, there would have been about thirty-five local people crammed on the back, not counting babies on the breast and dogs. But fair enough, no one wanted to miss out on the big weekend.

It was standing room only as we headed on down the track. I was doing it tough crammed in the back, and to make it worse one bloke decided to try and have a leak while we were travelling. He had the right idea, trying to shoot it over the edge of the trayback, but because of the speed we were going it just came spraying back on everybody. I wore most of it and I was starting to feel a bit jaded.

We finally made town late afternoon sometime. We dropped off the mob and poked on over to the showground, about half a kilometre from the pub. All the station people were camped around there, and us young blokes were expected to help set Old Morris and his missus up, get them firewood and stuff like that, and be good ambassadors for the station.

It wasn't difficult to work out that the grog wasn't going to flow in this camp. It would be billy tea and sandwiches with no one sowing any wild oats. So I figured it was time to get organised and get my arse over to the pub. I got my swag out of the Toyota and put it in the fork of a tree, then told everyone I was off to make a few phone calls and I'd see them in a minute. I headed off down the track with my pay cheque smouldering away in my pocket like a hot coal. I couldn't wait to extinguish it.

On the way I passed the showground. The mob there looked as if they were getting ready for a big night at the hall. There were balloons going up, women and kids poking around, and I think there was some kind of function on there later, something to do with the race meeting. But it was probably going to be a real family affair and Morris and the gang would probably be there. So I kept on walking down the road a bit. I knew by intuition the place to be was the little pub — and I couldn't have been more right.

The joint was rockin. The first beer went down so well it brought tears to my eyes and I nearly passed out. It was a great atmosphere, everyone yarning, mostly stockmen from various stations catching up. It wasn't long before I was mixing in and chatting with blokes. The old rabbit-trapper I'd met before was partaking, so I had a beer with him. He'd been doing it hard but had made a bit of beer money. I forgot all about Morris, I forgot all about everything. I was just enjoying the cold beer. The hours flew by. The jukebox was getting a fair shake-up, with Slim Dusty and the same Charlie Pride song getting selected over and over. Everyone was singing along and taking on freight like there was no tomorrow.

I was having the time of my life. It was getting on towards midnight and I had progressed onto rum and gone into second gear feeling pretty good. A few blokes had already choked out, slumped here, slumped there, and the old rabbiter looked about set to astral travel any minute, but all in all spirits were still high. Looking around the bar I noticed one girl I thought was checking me out. So I take another quick look around and, sure enough, she's smiling at me. I returned the smile and tried to look cool. Every time I looked over she was looking my way, but she seemed to be with a bloke.

Wouldn't that shit you, I'm thinking, last girl left in the bar and she thinks I'm all right, but she's got a boyfriend hanging off her. Oh well, that's how it goes. So I hopped into my rum for a while and did a bit more singing and carrying on with the blokes I'd met. All's not lost, I thought, it had been a great night anyway.

A bit later, just out of curiosity, I looked around to see what she was up to and to my surprise her boyfriend had passed out drunk and was curled up at her feet, choked down like an old dog, totally out of it. Very interesting, I'm thinking.

I ordered another rum, took another look, and the girl's smiling right at me, then looking down at him, then smiling back at me. She did this a couple of times, like she was trying to tell me something. Now my blood pressure's going up. It's going right up. If it goes up any more, my head's going to shoot clean off, I thought. I couldn't work out why she'd zeroed in on me. I'm no oil painting, hadn't had a wash for a few days, was caked in dust from the ride in and smelled like stale urine!

She was making eyes now. This was getting serious. Waves of passion, like an electric current, were washing up and down my body. Then she casually up and walked out in the direction of the outside dunny. Faint heart ne'er won fair maiden, I said to myself as I decided to head out to the loo as well, hoping to run into her and maybe start a bit of a conversation or something.

I had no idea what was about to take place.

She came out of nowhere and we went into a clinch.

After every bit of oxygen had been drained out of me, we finally unplugged for a breath, then hooked straight back up like a set of uni-joints. There was no time for conversation. We were somewhere in the shadows between the pub and the outside dunny and things were happening pretty quick. We'd already crossed the line from passion and we were starting to head in the direction of reckless abandon. So I put the brakes on for a minute and suggested we walk back to the campground where my swag was located and maybe chew the fat there for a while.

She was all for it. As we walked, we talked a bit. She was a governess, just come in for the race meeting. So on we strolled, whispering, cooing, purring, kissing, clinching, until somewhere between the showground and the campground it all got too much and we started to get it on then and there.

Unfortunately, the function at the showground had come to an end at about the same time we decided to kick off. People were getting in their vehicles, ready to poke off down the track back to the campground with no idea that Romeo and Juliet would be going nineteen to the dozen on the side of the road in full view.

Up the road they came, all doing about 10 kilometres an hour. There must have been twenty or thirty vehicles heading back to the campground. When the procession approached I thought, bloody hell! I hadn't counted on this! What's a bloke meant to do? But it was too late, they were on us, high-beams flashing, horns beeping, wolf whistles, screams, kids yelling, the full bloody bit!

I glanced at one vehicle and saw a woman trying to cover her kids' eyes. Next thing I knew Old Morris went cruising past, sitting in the passenger seat of some Toyota, smoke hanging off his bottom lip, staring straight at me. He looked totally dumbfounded and did a double-take. Then his wife stuck her head out the same window, mouth wide open as they sailed past. Morris sucked so hard on his rollie the orange glow illuminated their faces and it looked like they'd gone straight into shock.

I realised it was probably one of the greatest love scenes of all time: somewhere between *Gone With the Wind* and *Debbie Does Dallas*. It also was at that precise moment I realised I'd just made a name for myself as a jackaroo. I was representing the station all right but not quite in the manner Old Morris and his wife had intended. Taking off, getting pissed and then the big Errol Flynn on the side of the road. It didn't look real good.

Anyway, we headed off for my swag and got set for Act Two. Somewhere down the line I must have passed out and she took off, because in the morning I woke up in bright daylight, completely naked, lying on top of my swag.

I sat up. To my horror, a crowd had formed. There's Old Morris, his missus and quite a mob of other people staring straight at me, pointing and carrying on. Their jaws seemed to be working overtime. Even Morris's seemed to be going up and down.

I was a jackaroo with a future all right, but not on Morris's station. So with my head hung low, I got dressed, rolled my swag and took off. I had a feeling the grass might be a little greener on the other side of the hill, so that's where I headed.

Heading West

There sure have been some legendary journeys across the frontiers of Australia. John McDouall Stuart, Leichhardt, Giles, Burke and Wills, Madigan, just to name a few. They took up the challenge and they fought the odds. These blokes had a burning desire to see what was on the other side of the hill, but things didn't always go as planned. Some of them never got to where they were going. Some never *knew* where they were going.

A lot of times they suffered from lack of funds and proper planning — when you think about it, a bit similar to me. Proper planning was never my strong point, but I think I had my hand on it the night I decided to head off from Darwin. Like great explorers before me I wasn't exactly sure what to expect . . . I was just going.

I was a young bloke probably born a hundred years too late. Up till then most of my adventures seemed to revolve around grog, girls and failed cattle station jobs, and sometimes all three at once. But I think I definitely had that pioneering streak. I was gunna open up the country . . .

No money, no spare tyre, no spare fuel, no food or water, and completely no idea.

I don't know to this day why I picked Perth. I didn't even know where it was. I just knew that if you headed west you'd have to come across it sooner or later. Just the sound of 'heading west' really appealed to me. You know, people would wonder where Phil O'Brien disappeared to, and they'd say, 'Oh, he headed west.' It had a great ring to it. I was young, free and stupid . . . and I was heading west.

As with great explorers before me I had full confidence in my beast of burden, a 1970 Datsun 1200. It wasn't much, a small step up from a camel — but John McDouall Stuart would have loved one.

All great explorers know careful storage of equipment is the key to success. Realising this, I took great care as to what singlets and shorts got thrown in the green garbage bag I was using for a suitcase. Another similarity between the great explorers and me was the 'Diary'. Any explorer worth his salt kept a diary, it's the equivalent of the black box on a modern-day aircraft. It doesn't matter how dead you are when they find you, as long as they know why and how, everyone seems to be happy.

The Datsun, which I'd just bought off a mate, would have been a real sporty little number in its heyday, but its heyday was long gone. When I left Darwin, the thing missed and backfired all the 330 kilometres down to Katherine. One out-of-tune carby would have been plenty, but this thing had three and they were really hopping into the fuel.

The doors kept flying open, so I had to rope them shut. No wonder I got this thing so cheap, I'm thinking. It was good in a shower of rain — only one windscreen wiper worked and that was on the passenger side. The gearbox was stuffed as well — I knew the gears were out there somewhere but I was buggered if I could find them. But apart from all its flaws, the Datsun kept going and that was good enough for me. So the diary for the first day was fairly uneventful:

Heading West Diary, Day One
Gearbox not worth three knobs of billygoat shit.

Day two proved a little more dramatic. After a restless night crashed in the back of the Datsun in the Crossways Hotel carpark I pulled up rough, but came good after a steakburger from the 24-hour. Now that's serious bush tucker.

With the sun getting higher and hotter by the minute, me and the Datsun backfired west. We travelled through the Victoria River district and on to Timber Creek, where I thought I'd rest the Beast of Burden and slide down a much-needed hair of the dog at the Timber Creek pub. Timber Creek was only a small place but it had plenty of the essential stuff.

I met a good sort of bloke there, can't quite remember his name, but he had two blue heeler dogs. One was called 'Bundy' and the other was called 'No Ice', and the three of them were travelling on a motorbike heading to Katherine. By the time they left the pub he was pretty cut, and I'm sure I saw No Ice steering as they shot past the pub window. Must have had a bit of guide dog in him.

Feeling refreshed, I pushed on west towards the border, the country changing with every spent kilometre, and me and the Beast of Burden slid into the East Kimberley full of anticipation. Statuesque boab trees dotted the landscape. These trees are a signature for the Kimberley country and they really add personality to the bush there.

So my spirits were high as I forked the mighty Datsun, heading out into the unknown. Money was low but it always had been. I suppose most exploration through history has been done on a tight budget. The Datsun's three untunable carbies seemed to be suffering manic mood swings. You'd get a good run for a while, then just when you thought it had settled down, bang, she'd start missing and surging. As I pulled into the servo at Kununurra the thing let rip with a backfire that made the whole main street look around, as if someone was shooting at them. The police across the road seemed fairly interested in the car's condition, so after fuelling up, I quit town.

The sky out to the west was starting to look ominous, chunky deep black clouds banking up. The weather was just about to turn violent, but nothing I couldn't handle, I thought.

Anyone with any real brains would have stayed put at this stage, because the weather up north in the wet season can really turn it on and it's not a good time for travelling. There wasn't a lot of traffic on the road either. Bugger all to be precise, just me and the Datsun on a voyage into the black. And black it was getting.

An hour or so down the track I came to a little roadside stop, not really a roadhouse, just a small cabin on the side of the road that sold a few odds and ends. But it wasn't open, because no one was travelling, except me. There was a sign nailed to a tree out the front that caught my eye. It read: 'We don't piss on your trees, so don't piss on ours.'

The sun slipped away and me and the Datsun were presented with a night blacker than the inside of a dead dog's guts. And you wouldn't have to perform long service at the weather bureau to work out it was going to really let go. Just as Highway One went from bitumen to dirt, it started to hammer down. Lightning forked its way through the blackness and I started to feel a little anxious. But probably no worse than John McDouall Stuart and the boys felt at Attack Creek.

Breaking new ground was always gunna be tough.

It didn't take long for the dirt road to turn to slush. The one saving grace was the Datsun's fat chunky tyres, which just managed to get enough traction to churn through the bog. After a while the road deteriorated even more with the torrential rain and I found myself only averaging about 10 kilometres an hour sliding through the night. The Beast of Burden was willing enough but these conditions were really testing the old girl. I was starting to realise what those early explorers had had to go through!

It was getting hard to see where I was going with only the passenger-side wiper working. It was either crane my neck over to that side or hang it out the window, but when I tried that I almost got my hair singed by a wild lightning fork. Then catastrophe nearly struck on a creek crossing, water bubbling up through the holes in the floor, just like a spring. The Datsun stalled and the water kept coming up and coming up, and old stubbies started to float free, and I thought it was the end of the line for this expedition. Almost time to grab my garbage bag suitcase, untie the rope holding the door shut and wade off.

But one last lean on the key and the Datsun dug deep and fired.

It may have been untuned, untimed, unkempt and unregistered, but the Datsun had guts and we crawled out of there. A short but descriptive excerpt from the diary indicates the mood and tension at the time.

Heading West Diary Night Two
Fuck this.

I slogged on for a few more hours then ran out of fuel. That was that. The storm cleared, which left me to cop an absolute pizzling from the local mozzies. I'd never seen them so fierce. They were even biting the Datsun. What a night! I'm sure I was down to my last pint of blood when the sun came up.

As the day got started you wouldn't even have known it had rained the night before, the country had just swallowed it up. I was pretty well unprepared. I had no water, no food, nothing. And the only traffic so far was an emu, and it was going the other way. By mid-morning I was as dry as a Wazubi tribesman's jockstrap. By midday my tongue felt like an unlicked saltlick. I wasn't quite at the stage where you drink your own urine, but I tell you what, I was looking around for a container.

By mid-afternoon I was starting to think I was going to turn out to be just another Australian pioneering statistic. Then a road train appeared in the shimmer of the heat haze away down the track. I would have smiled but my lips wouldn't move. So I just stood there next to the fagged-out Datsun, looking like a half-cooked mud crab. As the road train got closer I could see it was pulling two trailerloads of cattle, double-deckers. The rig finally rattled up and ground to a stop. The cattle bawling away on the back were swallowed up in a veil of dust.

To this day I reckon the driver was pissed. He was sitting up in the cab grinning away like a feral cat that had just eaten the last endangered marsupial.

'You got a drink, mate? I'm perished.'

Without the smile leaving his face he tossed down a hot can of beer, near on gearbox temperature. By the look of things that's probably what he'd been sucking on the whole trip. I clawed the top off and tipped it straight in. It went down all right but somewhere between my throat and my stomach it turned to froth, did a U-turn and headed straight back up, much to the truckie's amusement. I went down on me knees having a good old gag, froth bubbling out of me nose, and through teary eyes I could see the truckie, smile still clamped on his dial, standing on the dirt now, this time with a water bottle.

We had a laugh and I told him my story. He offered me a tow to the next town. Out comes the towrope — all of about six feet of it — the truckie still grinning away like a reef shark. So before I knew it there we were, rolling down the track, one half-pissed truckie, two double-decker trailerloads of bullocks, six feet of rope and me in the Datsun. My diary entry reads:

Heading West Diary Day Three
Getting skull-dragged down track by road train. Driver half pissed. Being severely shat on by bullocks.

She was a wild trip, dust pouring up through the holes in the floor, gravel showering the windscreen — the only time I could see was when the Datsun got pissed on by a bullock. Burke and Wills never had to go through this, I'm thinking. A bloke needed nerves of steel. If the truckie had had to hit the skids for some reason, me and the Datsun would have ended up in the back with the cattle, and it wouldn't have been pretty either. Anyway, after a few long hours of driving dust and catapulting cattle dung we finally made the bitumen. Old Smiley unhooked me at a little town called Fitzroy Crossing.

I fuelled up with my last few bucks and was on my way. The Datsun, mudguard hanging off and windscreen a little cobwebby, was looking a bit the worse for wear, but we relentlessly pushed on west. Me and the Datsun might have suffered from lack of funds, lack of planning, lack of know-how and lack of just about everything else, but like those great men before us, Charles Sturt, Ludwig Leichhardt, Burke and Wills and Slim Dusty, we had endurance, there was bloody no doubt about it. We were in for the long haul.

So we ate up the long boab-speckled miles on to the Western Australian coastal town of Broome. Confident, undaunted. Like all great explorers, I felt pride swell up inside me as I rolled into town, a major leg of the journey completed. I wasn't sure how much further Perth was, but it had to be somewhere down the track, I reasoned. After all, we were on the Western Australian coast! I thought I'd chuck a lap around the town just to take it all in, you know, soak up the moment, just as any other great explorer of the past would have done.

Big mistake.

A cop came out of nowhere, pulled me over and slapped a defect notice on the Datsun. He told me that the car was in that bad a state, that if it had been a horse he would have had to take it out the back and shoot it.

The Datsun, R.I.P.

It was a cruel blow. Disaster had struck the expedition. Under the advice of the local police I drove the Beast of Burden straight down the road to Broome Wreckers, where it was laid to rest, never to be seen again.

With a tear in my eye I pocketed the one hundred dollars from the wreckers. They reckoned if it hadn't been for the fat tyres I wouldn't even have got that much. I sat in the cool shade on the verandah of the Continental Hotel, reflecting that it was a sad day in Australia's exploration history, no doubt about it.

But I also realised one very interesting point: in the old days when the beast of burden died on the trail, the explorers would eat it and so gain some satisfaction from it, even in death. As I slowly sipped into the hundred dollars, I reckoned things hadn't changed that much . . .

The Duponts — All the Way from Paris

The Duponts were a couple of your regular everyday multi-millionaires from Paris, and all they wanted was a nice quiet holiday in Australia. They were sick of the Riviera, and the south of Spain was getting so crowded, and Club Med Monaco, well, that would always be there next year, so why not sip a few cocktails at some exclusive resort in sunny Australia, they reckoned. Nothing too strenuous. Maybe venture out of the air-con in the late afternoon and hold a koala or, if they were feeling adventurous, have a real outdoors experience like a game of golf.

Everything would have been all right except for the fact that someone sold them the wrong trip. Some travel agent must have stuffed up when they got to Australia — their English was pretty bad so I'd say that's where the misunderstanding took place. Instead of going to some ritzy country club they ended up getting sent to a remote Kimberley cattle station where I was working. And this place was bloody rough as guts — I didn't even know what I was doing there!

I couldn't believe it when the boss of the station called up and said, 'There's two French millionaires on the way. Go and meet them at the river.' Of course the boss wasn't living there, he had more brains than that, the joint was too rough even for him. There wasn't much cattle work either because all the cattle had run off — the place was too rough for them as well. There were just a few silly bastards like me living there who had nowhere else to go in the middle of the wet season.

Rivers were flooding, it was stinking hot, humidity was up to 193 per cent and there was a snake on every corner, not to mention the rats, scorpions and stuff. Why the hell would two millionaires from Paris want to experience this? I was pulling out myself as soon as the rivers went down. I was sick of dodging snakes, sick of dodging crocs and sick of dodging rats.

The boss rang back to make sure we got the message right: 'Two French tourists: pick up: river: sunset.'

'Yeah, got that, yeah, got that. And yeah, we'll look after them.'

What the hell was going on, we wondered. I knew the boss had planned to try and get a few tourists up here in the dry season, but that was a long way off. Not your everyday tourists either, probably four-wheel-drive enthusiasts or fishermen, adventure tourists. It was too far between cocktails for the up-market mob.

I hooked up the little boat trailer and headed off through the hills, slowly winding down to the river which was a bloody raging, roaring torrent about half a kilometre wide. The boss had apparently hired someone to drive the millionaires out from Kununurra Airport after they'd flown in from Sydney. From there it was about a three-hour drive to the river. I was to go across the river in the tinny and ferry them back, then take them up to the station for their relaxing holiday in paradise.

One look at the river and I'm thinking, I hope they're good swimmers if something goes wrong.

I could see them on the other side, two figures dressed completely in white. From a distance they looked like two boundary umpires. I'm thinking, that's ambitious wearing white in this country. As I launched the 10-foot dinghy into the water I was feeling a little toey myself — there were logs and branches and all sorts of stuff eddying around, not to mention the odd floating handbag or two (otherwise known as crocodiles). A bloke could come unstuck here very easily.

The water was rushing too fast for me to go directly across so I had to head downstream, edge across bit by bit and then come up the other side into the current. The two figures in white didn't seem to be moving much. They looked rigid and were just staring at the river. It probably took me a good fifteen minutes to get across and as I came closer I couldn't help but do a double-take at the Duponts. They looked absolutely pristine, everything about them was bloody immaculate. They must have been pedicured, manicured, facialled, waxed, polished, nipped and tucked ... and they were totally colour coordinated.

I pulled in and yelled, 'Gidday, gidday. How goes it?' But no reply. The Duponts were in shock. They just stared through me at the river. The bloke that had dropped them off gave me a wink and said, 'I'll see you back here in a week.' He took off and I could see he was pissing himself laughing.

The Duponts looked terrified. The old boy couldn't speak any English at all and she could only speak a little bit. They started mumbling and carrying on but it was hard to hear them above the roar of the river. I tried to explain that we had to go as it was getting dark and very dangerous, but I think they'd worked that one out for themselves.

I gestured to Mrs Dupont to get in the dinghy and it was like I'd asked her to walk the plank or something. I finally got her in, but getting the old boy in was like trying to coax a cat down from a tree. The worst thing that can happen in a small dinghy is that if someone moves suddenly to one side, the boat can tip over before you know it. I didn't have to worry with the Duponts, they wedged themselves in and they never moved an inch. Their knuckles were glowing white from gripping the side of the tinny. They were petrified by the wide, surging, screaming river.

On the other side I had to carry Mrs Dupont from the boat to dry land as she didn't want to get her designer footwear wet. Fair enough, I'm thinking, but then the old boy pulls the same stunt and I had to carry him as well. Perhaps it's an old French tradition. We tried to communicate a bit on the way back to the station. They seemed concerned as to where I was taking them. I tried to keep them relaxed but they were really wound up, as though we were heading to a work camp in Siberia.

They certainly weren't in a festive holiday mood.

Back at the station I showed them their room. They couldn't believe it. They looked as if they'd just gone to jail for something they didn't do.

Admittedly the rooms were rough — walls and roof of rusty corrugated iron and stone floors. Not much effort had gone into making the floors level — walking into one of those rooms was like walking up a creek bed. I showed them where the mozzie coils were and left them to it.

The Duponts' first night of their holiday could have been smoother but we tried our best. As it was an extremely hot and sticky night, we'd put them in a room where the corrugated iron wall didn't quite meet the corrugated iron roof, with a gap of about a metre between them. I thought the room might be a bit breezier for them, plus it had a good ceiling fan.

This was all great in theory, till in the middle of the night a fruit bat flies in and gets chopped to pieces by the ceiling fan, followed later on by another one. This was quite common — I think all that corrugated iron must have upset the inbuilt radar of the bats somehow — but try telling that to two distraught French millionaires.

I really felt sorry for them, they must have been up all night by the look of them and they wanted out.

I explained that the airstrip at the station was under water and the only way out was the way they came in, across the river, but that the bloke from Kununurra wouldn't be back for a week. So they moped around like they were next in line for the electric chair.

The next drama was the outdoor shower. Mr Dupont was scrubbing up when a giant green tree frog jumped onto his back. He nearly screamed the place down. Then the old girl went to use the dunny and she started screaming. One of the dogs had dragged a snake in there and was chewing on it. For us, all this stuff was normal.

It was one thing after the other, and by late in the day everyone was ready for a drink, including me. So we sat around in the cool of the afternoon and gave the Duponts a couple of stiff ones. We soon worked out there had been a big mistake with their holiday arrangements. We sympathised, and yarned as best we could, considering the language problem, and things were settling down nicely. They didn't seem like bad folks. With a couple more drinks and a few laughs, you could almost say they started to relax — not quite, but almost.

Then a beautiful little crimson finch turned up and the Duponts became really excited by this exquisite bird. So they're checking it out and I'm thinking, they're starting to loosen up, good on you, finch. But out of nowhere dropped a python and within a split second it was squeezing the life out of the bird. The Duponts became hysterical. The snake was trying to swallow it, so one bloke got the shotgun and unloaded on the snake. KABOOM! He missed and shot a hole in the wall. The snake dropped the bird and fell on the ground at the feet of the Duponts, who freaked. One of the dogs ran in, swallowed the finch and ran off, leaving the snake still wriggling around. Mr Dupont was tap-dancing and the old girl tried to get on a table.

I finally frightened the snake off with a stick, but the poor buggers were really rattled. We sat them down and pumped a few more drinks into them. Mrs Dupont was so wound up she looked down at the designer logo on the pocket of her top and went crazy, brushing at it with her hand, screaming — she thought it was something crawling up her shirt. When she realised it was just a logo she calmed down a bit.

That night the boss rang up and asked how it was going. I told him it wasn't. He made out to be a bit surprised but he reluctantly agreed to try and get the guy out from Kununurra a few days early. He said he'd be in touch.

The Duponts got through another night. They didn't use the ceiling fan, figuring it was better to sweat it out than get showered with bat guts again. Apart from two bush rats mating under the bed, it was a pretty quiet night.

The next day someone came up with an idea to take them on an outing to a local waterfall — maybe have a BBQ and boil the billy, give them a paddle in one of the rock pools. It was a stinking hot day but it looked like the rain might hold off at least, so we loaded them into a four-wheel drive with some meat and stuff for the day, and a bloke who knew the area pretty well volunteered to take them. They seemed happy enough when they left. Maybe this could be the turning point, I'm thinking, maybe this could be the day they decide the outback isn't such a bad place after all. So feeling good, I set about catching up on a few jobs around the place. I decided I'd do a rubbish run in the old tractor, so I grabbed as much rubbish as I could find and loaded it in the bucket of the tractor.

I suppose it had been a good two hours since the Duponts had left for their big day out. No doubt they were out there somewhere having fun, probably splashing around in a beautiful rock pool. I poked off in the old tractor heading for the dump, bouncing along the road, sun beating down. I turned a corner and there staggering down the track were the Duponts!

Their designer-coordinated outfits were caked with sweat and mud and they were stuffed, barely getting one foot in front of the other. I reckon another hour in the sun and they would have been dead. Mrs Dupont staggered up to the tractor, her face like a tomato and her lips like two dried apricots, and she says, 'Le bog, le bog, le bog.' Then the old boy started up, 'Le bog', and waving his arms around.

Apparently they'd gone about ten kilometres and the bloke driving had pulled off the road to show them an old set of cattle yards and they'd got bogged up to the doors in mud. The driver was still back there digging it out. The Duponts thought they could walk back as there was no shade out there. Well, 10 kilometres goes forever when you're not used to the heat, as they found out. They flopped in the tractor's bucket with all the rubbish and I headed home. If only the Paris mob could see them now, I'm thinking. Choked down in the bucket amongst the garbage, bouncing down the road in the old station tractor. They were a real mess, covered in mud and on their last legs.

Back at the station the Duponts lay low. I felt sorry for them — all they'd wanted was a quiet holiday. I was bloody thankful the boss came good and organised the bloke from Kununurra to be at the river a few days sooner. When I told them we could get them out early, their faces lit up and they nearly broke down and wept.

So we crossed the mighty river again. The Duponts hung on so tight that when we got to the other side they had aluminium wedged under their fingernails. Once again I had to lift Mrs Dupont out onto the dry ground and same with the old boy. I don't blame him — his designer slip-ons probably cost him more than I was making in a month at the Last Frontier Holiday Centre for Wayward French Millionaires. We said our goodbyes and they pleaded with me to come with them, to get away from this place. They meant well and I told them I wouldn't be far behind them, once the river went down. And as they took off I thought, yeah, you got it, mate, the sooner I get out of this place the better — and that's for le bloody sure!'

Tall in the Saddle

Not long ago I was having a few quiet ones at one of my favourite little watering holes, the Kulgera Pub in Central Australia. It's a sentimental spot for me as it's been the backdrop for a few interesting encounters, failed romances and the odd job dismissal or two. It's a place I like to go to so I can get in touch with my inner self, meditate and reconnect — or in other words, drink with the locals.

Like other spiritual destinations, Kulgera Pub has been the focal point of many a pilgrimage. After six months straight on an outlying cattle station I once made the journey and drank for three days solid. Now that's not heavy drinking, it's just what you'd call making up for lost time.

The property I was working on was an interesting place. It was one of those places time forgot. If you'd seen the place in 1880 then went back in 1980 you'd notice nothing had changed. And things were done the same way they'd always been done — the hard way!

The stock camp was mostly made up of local Aboriginal stockmen, and me. And I was a real asset — not being good at anything, I was the source of entertainment for everyone. My day would start at about three-thirty in the morning when I'd have to walk off with the horse-tailer and try and find the plant of working horses. As there were bugger all yards and fences, the horses would be hobbled at the end of the day's mustering and let go. They'd cover miles during the night, feeding, and so me and Johnny the horse-tailer would cover miles at three-thirty in the morning looking for them. A cowbell was usually hung around a quiet horse's neck, so if you were lucky you could sometimes zero in on its rattle. But young Johnny had grown up with these horses and he pretty well always knew where they'd be.

As we covered the miles, walking along in the dark with our bridles, Johnny would often try and scare me with stories of Featherfoot, the bloke that points the bone. And if that didn't get me looking over my shoulder he'd throw in a few ghost stories, or a murder that took place 'just over there by that rock'.

'They speared him ten times!' he'd explain.

'OK, Johnny.'

'And then they cut his . . .'

'OK, Johnny.'

'. . . and then the dingoes . . .'

'OK . . . thanks, Johnny.'

Every morning was the same, and I'd usually be jumpy as shit by the time we found the horses. Then the fun would really start.

A lot of horses slept standing up but a fair few would lie down as well, and every horse Johnny went up to and woke would just slowly open its eyes and have a bit of a stretch. Johnny would talk to them quietly in Aboriginal, and it was all very relaxed.

I don't know why, but I got a completely different response from the horses that I woke up. They'd jump up, go mad and run off. I'm sure I actually made our jobs harder, but Johnny, like many Aboriginal people, just loved to laugh, and I provided him with some good ones.

The unwritten law for horse-tailers is that — no matter what — the horses must be back at the camp ready for work before first light, because by the time you get that first bit of light you should be saddled up, ready to get out there and start mustering. Not many station bosses like it if they can't squeeze at least fourteen hours a day out of you.

So once we'd got the horses going, we'd race them back to the camp, bareback. I'd usually come riding in somewhere down round the belly with Johnny pissing himself at me. Bareback wasn't one of my strong points. Then it was a cup of tea, some damper, catch a horse, saddle up and start the day. Everyone had three to four horses allotted to them, so you'd rotate them a bit, maybe ride one for the morning then change horses at lunchtime, and the next day ride a different one again. This kept the horses in reasonable condition and they wouldn't get too knocked up.

My four working horses weren't exactly the cream of the crop. One of them was so old it could barely crack a fart. One had mastered the art of trotting and cantering backwards. One was an ex-show jumper, so no matter what you were doing it just wanted to jump — one minute you're trying to wheel some bullock, next thing the horse bolts off and jumps a bush, then prances around thinking it's going to get a ribbon. I just couldn't control it. My last horse not only had a mind of its own, it had several minds of its own. It was schizophrenic.

Most of the other horses were pretty good, but everyone else was riding them.

Johnny didn't come out mustering much during the day because the horse-tailer was responsible for the fifty or so horses in the plant. He'd make sure they were on a bit of good feed somewhere and that they stayed in good nick, and he treated them like family.

So the day would begin with me selecting a horse from my star-studded line-up. The old horse was fine in the morning — he was easy to catch and you'd slip the bit in between his grey whiskery old lips and he'd just hang his head down and you'd plod off. You had to stay a bit sharp on him though, because at any moment he could just lie down and die and you wouldn't want to get trapped underneath him. The ex-show jumper had a bit more gas and used to jump clear out of the camp, with everyone laughing at my total lack of control over it. I think its best jump was a 44-gallon drum, but I wasn't on it at the time — it did that one by itself while I was running after it.

I dreaded the mornings I'd have to ride the horse that trotted backwards. We'd all ride off from the camp in the direction we were going to muster and once we were about 100 metres from the camp he'd stop. Then he'd start walking backwards and I'd kick him but it made no difference, and when he got a bit of momentum up he'd get into a trot and then with a bit more speed he'd break into a canter, still going backwards. He obviously didn't want to leave the other horses. Not only did it look funny, it was a really strange sensation. The other blokes would have to ride back and hunt him from behind with sticks. It was pretty embarrassing stuff. Once you got him a mile or so away from the camp he'd settle down, but it was a huge joke for everyone — except me.

My last horse, the schizophrenic, was definitely the most dangerous for a bloke with my lack of ability. You really needed to have your wits about you when you got on him in the morning. As soon as your arse hit the saddle he'd bolt uncontrollably for a good mile or so and it was hard getting any control over him. He almost killed both of us one morning when he bolted off, heading straight for a cliff. As hard as I tried I couldn't pull him up. He obviously wanted to end it all. The cliff was coming up fast, and this horse would've kamikaze-ed straight off the edge if it hadn't been for Johnny galloping up alongside and reaching over to grab the reins and help pull him up. It was a very courageous thing to do, but Johnny just laughed his head off. I got wise after that and made sure the horse was pointing in the right direction before I got on.

No one else seemed to have the problems I did, but then they were all pretty seasoned and I was probably lacking a bit of confidence. Without a doubt the mornings were always entertaining — and I was usually at the centre of it all.

Anyway, at first light we'd poke off to whatever area we'd planned to muster. The days were long and hard, searching for mobs of cattle, pushing them together and covering a lot of country. It was pretty challenging because there wasn't a lot of water about and drinks were few and far between. Sometimes you'd stop for lunch if it worked out that you weren't far from the camp, otherwise you'd go all day.

The Aboriginal blokes I worked with on this place were really good and they took to stock work as if it was an extension of their own culture. But one day I showed them some real style, something they'll never forget, something that will be talked about around campfires for many years to come. An electrifying, explosive, dynamic performance. Man and beast, a bloke and his horse united as one . . .

A mob of cattle had been mustered and pushed onto an open flat area and Bingy, the head stockman, had decided to cut out all the bullocks from the mob. A fair bit of skill is involved in cutting out, it's a real art. A bloke on a good horse that's trained for cutting out works his way through the mob and on locating a bullock or whatever he intends to cut out from the mob, sets his horse to it and the horse shoulders it out. It's an age-old way of doing things and to see a good man like Bingy on a well-trained enthusiastic horse cutting out is pretty impressive. There was no better man than Bingy for this type of work, he knew horses and cattle like no other. He was a master.

Bingy the Master on a bull. He was the only one who could get near it.

So there were about six or seven hundred head in the mob with about four blokes holding them and Bingy doing the cutting out. Once he'd got a bullock out, someone else would hunt it over to me and my job was to hold all of them in a little mob. I was riding the old pensioner that day and he was going even worse than usual. He seemed really stiff-legged and his tongue was hanging out the side of his mouth. But we'd been trusted with the important task of holding the bullocks and we were at last getting some recognition as important members of the team.

The old horse farted, stumbled and nearly fell over as we prowled around the growing group of about thirty bullocks, and it looked like there were still a fair few more to get cut out and come our way. Now I don't know if it's been scientifically proven or not, but cattle undoubtedly have telepathic powers. I've seen it. One minute the whole lot of them were just standing there staring up at me, and I was staring down at them, then without as much as a single 'moo' they pissed off in complete unison. They took off across the flat at a full gallop. Some of them were up on their back legs running like goannas. Then they ran up a hill and disappeared in a cloud of dust. I sunk the spurs into Old Horse ready for the fiery chase. He just hung his head and farted. He wasn't chasing anyone anywhere. He stood there like a stale bottle of piss and for a moment I thought he'd died standing up, but he blurted out another tremendous fart and I knew he was still alive.

Bingy saw what had happened and took off after them. He was across the flat and over the hill in no time at all, and I could see the flash of his white teeth as he laughed. He was gone for a full ten minutes, and me and the old pensioner horse hadn't moved. Then some dust appeared over the hill and sure enough down came the bullocks with Bingy right up their arse, giving them a flick with his whip, and he landed them right back at the spot they'd taken off from, directly in front of me and the old horse. It was a mighty ride by Bingy, but he thought it was a great joke, as did everyone else.

The Aboriginal blokes on that place had a fantastic sense of humour and we worked well together. And as I said earlier, I was a real asset, giving them plenty to laugh about. And there were days on that place I'll always hold dear to my heart, and on my death bed I hope it's the memory of sitting behind a mob of cattle with those blokes that drifts across my mind and is my last vision on this earth. Working and living with men like Bingy and Johnny was a real education and they inspired me to go on and get more cattle station jobs in the future. But one time up in the Kimberley it was that inspiration that nearly got me killed.

I'd got a job on a station that was gearing up for its first muster of the year. Now this can be a pretty exciting time on a property, as most of the working horses haven't been ridden for four or five months. They come in fresh and generally with a bit of attitude.

Aladdin came in fresh all right *and* with plenty of attitude — and believe me, it was all bad. He was a big, strong, good-looking horse. He looked like he had a bit of breeding in him and I think this is what had saved him, otherwise I'd say someone would have shot him years before. When I first saw him in the paddock I couldn't help but notice his good looks. He moved really well.

A bit long in the leg maybe, but he sure looked like he could go. Of course I was new on the place and I didn't know the history of the horse. I had no idea of the pain and suffering he'd instilled in the heart of many a bloke before me. But it dawned on me something was amiss the day the head stockman was allocating horses. I ended up with Aladdin and all the other blokes cracked up laughing. Then this old Aboriginal bloke makes the sign of the cross and they all crack up again! A thought entered my mind, flashing like a neon sign: 'Mongrel horse ... mongrel horse ... and you're stuck with it!' Every station had a few, and it was usually the new bloke that got lumbered with them. The older blokes were too cunning.

I could see from the outset I was really going to earn my money on this place. We brought all the horses in and yarded them at the homestead yards. The idea with horses that have been spelled for a while is to get them in and ride them and handle them for a bit, get them used to the idea it's working time again. Just as people have their little differences, so do horses. Some go along with you and are quiet, you can jump straight on them, no worries. Others will do anything to keep you and the saddle off their back. And then there's ones like Aladdin that just plain have murder on their mind.

The other blokes started catching their particular horses and trying to get the saddles on and it was the usual sideshow — people swearing, horses bolting, dust, dust and more dust. This sort of atmosphere can unsettle a horse even more, so I cut Aladdin out of the mob and hunted him into a small holding yard by himself. He was flighty, kicking out like some kind of martial arts expert, nostrils flaring, tail stuck up in the air, prancing around the yard, wild as shit.

I let him go for a minute hoping he'd puff himself out a bit. Round and round he went. I grabbed the bridle and cornered him, and to my surprise and relief he was easy to catch and I had no trouble slipping the bridle on him. Next step was the saddle blanket. As I went to slip it on he turned and bit me fair in the back, then spun around and cow-kicked me in the shoulder. I went down like a ton of bricks. The cooperation between man and beast was over.

I was pulling myself out of the dirt when the head stockman came over — he'd obviously just recovered from a heavy bout of laughing.

Aladdin was prancing around victorious, reins dragging in the sand. Together we managed to catch him and get the saddle on his back — no mean feat with Aladdin striking out with his front hoofs like someone shadow-boxing.

This was it. Time to show him who's boss. I recited the Lord's Prayer and leapt on. He went berserk — he raked, he twisted, he bucked and he rooted. This horse had a red-hot coal up his arse and he was trying to send me to the moon. I stuck with him for as long as I could but he ended up spearing me straight back into the dirt. So flat on my back and only half conscious, I opened my eyes and there's Aladdin standing over me looking down through the dust.

The head stockman helped me to my feet. He was weak from laughing so much. Great, I thought, if I break my neck in this yard at least everyone's had a good laugh!

Back onto Aladdin I sprang. This time I was really pissed off and I stuck to him like shit to a blanket. He couldn't budge me. He twisted and spun and hopped all over the place but I was still on. So old Aladdin had to dig a bit deeper into his repertoire of tricks, and so he rubbed me along the rails of the yard till he finally scraped me off, sending me down into the dirt once again. The dust cleared and there he was looking straight down at me again — the horse from hell.

The head stockman came up grinning and said, 'You got him beat, old mate, you got him beat.'

I said, 'Thanks, that's great, but can you go tell the horse that?'

I think I cracked a rib when he jammed me up against the rails, but pain or no pain this horse wasn't going to beat me. I decided to hobble his front legs to restrict his movements a bit — an old trick but all's fair in love and war and horses. So on I got again. This time I had him. He performed but the hobbles slowed him up a bit. Around the yard we went and it seemed Aladdin was settling down. The next step with a horse like this, once you've taken the edge off it, is to take it out of the yard for a bit of a run out on the flat. A bit of a canter, turning him this way, then that, you know, some discipline.

Well, the hobbles came off and the gate was opened.

Aladdin didn't just trot out, you couldn't even say he galloped out, it was like he was fired out of a cannon — he bloody rocketed out. He screamed out across the flat going as fast as any horse has ever gone in the history of mankind. And I couldn't pull him up. I tried everything. So much for discipline. This horse was doing exactly what he wanted — I just happened to be on his back at the time!

Then Aladdin played his trump. He hit the skids. The bastard went from about 227 kilometres per hour to

'This Phil guy can't ride for shit.'
'I know. Where do they find them?'

nothing. But I stuck to the saddle this time, I was glued on, he wasn't gunna beat me. I stuck to that saddle all right, but hey . . . why the hell am I sailing through the air then? Something was wrong. I shouldn't be flying and still be in the bloody saddle!

Then . . . *hervoompah!* . . . me and the saddle sprawled in the dirt in an untidy heap, feeling sorry for ourselves. Shitbags had taken off, he probably thought he *had* killed me this time, so I wouldn't be much fun anymore.

The head stockman pulled up in an old Toyota laughing his head off. He said to have a bit of a rest and then we'd catch him and give it another go. 'You almost had him,' he kept saying. 'You almost had him!'

I've always found it hard to talk when I'm concussed and half-buried in the ground with a saddle on top of me, but I think my reply went something along the lines of, 'You fuckin' ride him!'

Thus ended the titanic battle between man and beast. As I was unceremoniously thrown in the back of the Toyota like a sack of spuds, I'm thinking, isn't it great in this day and age of rapidly developing technology to still be able to make a dollar sitting on the back of a horse? It's really something special . . .

Collecting Crocodile Eggs

You say to yourself, you'll never catch me doing that! Or, no way, mate! Then one day, you wake up and there you are, doing something that quite frankly was not in the game plan. And that's how I found myself in one of the most dangerous occupations around — farming saltwater crocodiles, not exactly what you'd call man's best friend.

This took place up in north-east Arnhem Land, a beautiful, wild and unique part of the Northern Territory. A cousin of mine was working with an Aboriginal community up there and he invited me up to have a look around any time I had the chance. I'd just finished a short stint at the Bungle Bungle National Park up the top of Western Australia, taking people on camping trips. It hadn't been a bad number — a little adventure combined with some great Australian scenery. The dry season, which is the time for travelling and exploring this part of the country, was now coming to an end and the wet season was coming up, so I weighed things up and decided to move on. The fact that I was working for a complete arsehole also had a bit to do with it, I suppose.

After about nineteen Emu Bitters at a not-so-quiet pub in Kununurra I felt pretty happy and was looking forward to whatever was coming up next, but with absolutely no idea that in a few short weeks I'd be doing a Crocodile Dundee in some swamp in Arnhem Land. But, unlike the movie, I'd be doing my own stunts and the crocs would be real (and I mean extremely bloody real).

I flew into the township of Nhulunbuy, situated in the top north-east corner of the Northern Territory. There was no chance of driving there at that time of year since the rivers and creeks were all on the way up with the early rains. I met up with my cousin, Paul, a likeable bloke in his forties. As per family tradition he had an esky full of cold beer, which helped us catch up with each other's yarns. He filled me in on the Aboriginal community he was involved with and the projects they had going, one of them being a crocodile farm. Great, I thought, nothing better than Aboriginal people trying to create some type of economic stability for the future. Paul assured me they were a pretty good mob up here, keen to stay traditional but also keen to hit the twenty-first century up and running economically.

We drove around as the monsoon rain started to slip down out of incredibly shaped clouds. It was a beautiful area, with woodlands full of stringy bark and cycad palms, pandanus clumped here and there, along with ironwood and woolly butt — beautiful contrasts of green against the red-ochred earth. Intoxicating. And intoxicated we were getting as we drove out in the direction of the community, Paul singing old Dean Martin songs and me just enjoying the scenery. What a great little holiday this is going to be, I was thinking. Bit of fishing, bit of drinking, bit more fishing . . .

The next few weeks were great. The community was situated on an exquisite part of coastline and there were fish everywhere, oysters on the rocks, crabs, clams, mussels — you name it, I ate it. The people were friendly and warm and I fitted in pretty good, making friends easily enough and just meandering around the joint.

The croc farm project seemed to be going OK. There were cages and ponds, incubators and, of course, crocs. Mostly ones that had been caught locally. A couple looked pretty toey, and you could see where they had been testing the fences trying to bust out. I wouldn't want one of them hanging off my arse, I thought as I moseyed around.

Paul was the Operations Manager and there was another white bloke who ran the day-to-day farm stuff, ably supported by a team of local Aboriginal blokes. As Paul pointed out, the farm was really geared up as a nursery — they planned to collect croc eggs from the wild, incubate them and, when they hatched, grow them up a little then sell them to other farms.

That's great, I thought, but what dickhead would go out in the swamps and flood plains of Arnhem Land and try and steal eggs from a pissed-off clucky croc? You'd never see that one advertised at Centrelink, that's for sure.

Life was pretty good all right. I dragged a few more coral trout onto the coals, ate about eighty dozen more oysters au naturel and enjoyed the odd cleansing ale or three. The sun came up, the sun went down, usually with splashes of intense colour stretching like fingers across the sky, turning all sorts of shades. Totally breathtaking. I was turning into a beach bum and loving it.

Then, as I fillet my first barramundi for the day, old Paul rocks up in a cloud of dust, gets out of his Toyota in a fluster and tells me he's had a falling out with the croc farm manager and the croc farm manager's done a Harold Holt. 'Shit, that's no good,' I said. 'Do you want a hand?' Paul reckoned that would be great, it would give him time to find another manager.

So for the next couple of weeks I was acting croc farm manager. No big deal, just keeping everything alive and fed, and joining in with the Aboriginal workers. As usual I went at it pretty hard, getting stuck into the place, cleaning it up, making the garden look good, mowing all the weeds and feeding the crocs up. I love animals and have a good head for that sort of stuff. I really hit it off with the boys working there, as well.

Maybe it was destiny, maybe it was fate, or more likely they couldn't find anyone else! But everyone was unanimous — they wanted me to stay on and run the farm. Now I can't resist a good challenge. All through my adult life I've been in situations where my brain is saying, 'Look, tell them to piss off, don't do it,' but my mouth always seems to say, 'Yeah, no worries, I'll have a go at that.' I usually end up in it up to my neck. This was no different. My brain lost out again and off I went.

Phil O'Brien, Croc Farmer! That's got a great ring to it, very important, very official, very distinguished. Of course I completely forgot the bit about collecting eggs in the wild. I was just swept away by the glory of the thing. I envisaged that in years to come there would be three names synonymous with crocodiles: Paul Hogan, Linda Koslowski and Phil O'Brien!

A week or so after my inauguration things were going great guns when the word came down the line: 'Meeting under the banyan tree at dinner time.' Well, there we were, under the banyan tree — Paul, the head bloke of the tribe, a few other men and me.

'Time to go for eggs. The Baru will be nesting now. Now is the time,' said the head bloke.

No problem, everyone agreed. I was thinking, who's going to be the dumb prick who goes and gets them, poor bugger. 'Great stuff,' I piped up. 'Let's fill those incubators with eggs and get this show on the road.'

Paul turned to me and said, 'We'll have a chopper coming from Katherine later this week and you and Stewy can head out and start collecting.'

Start collecting? Start collecting? Hey, are you talking to me? I was thinking.

I looked around. He was! I was the man all right. Good old Phil. Great guy, top bloke. But a 'gator got him — I could see the headstone. My brain tried to cut in with, 'Pull out, pull out, it's not too late', but unfortunately my lips had already formed the syllables, 'Yeah, no worries, I'll have a go at that.'

Now stealing eggs from crocs is probably on a par with going over Niagara Falls in a 44-gallon drum. Theoretically it's possible to survive, but if you didn't make it no one would be surprised. Life would go on and you'd just end up as croc shit, floating down the river, no problem.

Stewy, my partner in all this, was a full-blood Aboriginal bloke in his thirties. A likeable bloke, his job was to look out for the mum while I got the eggs out of the nest. There was only one problem: we weren't going to take a gun, as the crocodile was a sacred totem to the people there. To shoot one wouldn't go down well, so our only protection was a 14-foot wooden paddle off someone's boat.

To put the icing on the cake, the Conservation Commission of the Northern Territory wanted me to fill out a questionnaire at every croc nest we found, as they were trying to gather data on crocodiles. Questions such as: What grass was the nest compiled of? How many eggs? Was the female present? Was she aggressive? The temperature, and so on . . . How does a bloke do all that with a croc tearing at his jugular? But there was no turning back now and, as I've said, I can't resist a good challenge.

So me and Stewy spent the next few days dropping 44s of aviation fuel in various locations out bush, as the chopper only had two hours' flying time on a tank. Using maps of various river systems we worked out which places we'd try out. Stewy knew this area really well and we marked down places he already knew where crocs nested. Most nesting areas were inaccessible by vehicle, which was the reason for hiring the helicopter.

We were aiming for a quota of two thousand eggs. A croc will lay between twenty and sixty eggs, so it would be a big effort to find enough nests to reach the target. This project was not one for the faint-hearted, and although I turned out to be the silly bugger going out to collect the eggs, I really wanted it to work for the community.

The helicopter finally arrived, flying all the way across from Katherine. The pilot was a good sort of bloke, named Mick, nicknamed Mick Dundee.

He introduced himself then said, 'And this is David', clutching at a knife hanging off his belt that looked more like a sword. I'd heard of Mick before and he had a good reputation as a pilot and prided himself on being pretty reliable. Between him and David, there wasn't much they couldn't handle. We planned our strategy for the following day, which happened to be a Friday . . . there's an old bush superstition, never start anything on a Friday. What the hell, I thought — I probably wouldn't be coming back in one piece anyway.

Our plan was to fly low over the Peter John flood plain and the neighbouring Cato River spotting the nests from the air. Then Mick would drop me and Stewy as close as he could to the nest. It all depended on how many trees and the type of bush that was around as to how close he could get with the chopper. If it was open ground, we were sweet; if it wasn't, we'd have to hike in from wherever Mick could land. The next day when the sun came up I wondered what I would be doing when it went down

Mick and Stewy in front of the helicopter.

again. Hanging off a cold can, I hoped, not going through the digestive system of some potential belt and matching handbag!

Mick Dundee was up at first light servicing the chopper, which, incidentally, had a pretty wild paint job — something like Bob Dylan might have flown around in back in the seventies. So there we were, all set and ready for the big day. I had my steel-capped boots on so at least my toes were protected. Our equipment was secured — two large eskies to put the eggs in, the 14-foot paddle for protection, a water container and a pack of Arnott's Family Assortment shoved under the seat. Mick kicked her in the guts and off we choppered . . .

I hate flying, but a helicopter's something else. Especially flying as low as Mick was. Across the bay we went, going that low I was thinking I should have brought a hand-line and some bait. We finally crossed the bay and headed out across the treetops, the country opening up beneath. It was so exhilarating I forgot all about my fear of flying. The scenery was magic. A bit further on we hit the flood-plain country that pans out from the Peter John River.

We saw flocks of birds — brolga, magpie geese, egrets, jabiru — and water buffalo so fat they could hardly raise a trot.

Mick backed off with the throttle as a likely bit of country came into view. Sure enough, there was a nest — a mound about 1 metre high and 3 or 4 metres around, grass and mud raked up and packed together, working like compost and generating just the right amount of heat to incubate the eggs deep inside. We were lucky, as the nest was out in the open and Mick could land quite close. From the air, the flood-plain grass only looked about a foot long, but once you actually got down amongst it, it was well over your waist and in some areas well over your head. Stewy was first out with the paddle, poking it around in front of him like a mine-detector. I had an esky, a thermometer and a clipboard complete with Conservation Commission data sheets.

We got to the nest fairly easily — the female wasn't to be seen, but her tracks were everywhere and you could bet she wasn't far away. There was plenty of tension as Stewy raked the grass with the paddle and I broke apart the nest. I got to the eggs and started taking the temperature and checking them out. I looked up at Stewy — he was leaning on the paddle, rolling a smoke, not a problem in the world. I slowly took each egg out and placed it in the esky, packing them in with some of the nest material. How the croc lays them is how they have to stay for the eighty days or so of incubation, no twisting or turning the eggs. So I put a mark with a pencil on the top of each egg, so we knew which way was up. A slow process.

With the eggs finally packed in the esky, we headed back to the chopper, climbed in, gave Mick the thumbs up and off we went looking for another one. This isn't going to be that hard, I thought, and what great scenery! No problem, no sweat . . . too easy.

It wasn't long before we spotted another one, this time in amongst some trees, so Mick dropped us a few hundred metres away in a clearing. Off we went again, Stewy with his paddle, me with the esky and clipboard. Piece of piss, I'm thinking, piece of piss. We pushed through the long grass in the direction of the nest and then things started to get sticky. We hit a bit of lush rainforest with vines everywhere and it was very hard to see any distance. To make it worse, the ground was getting really boggy and I was starting to get a little bit of a twitch around the old clacker valve from walking in slush up to my knees.

We finally saw the nest in a bit of a clearing. So far no croc, so I thought we were home and hosed. When I was about 10 metres from the nest, I hit a pocket of real soft stuff and sank straight down up to my neck and couldn't move. Stewy was skimming along in front like a mudskipper, totally unaffected, but I would have been nearly double his weight. I was feeling a little nervous with just my head sticking out of the mud like some type of hors d'oeuvre. If the mum bolted out of somewhere right now, I'd be stuffed. She'd just bite my head clean off and say thanks for coming.

It's times like this you are meant to see your life flash before you, but I closed my eyes and all I could see was a Jatz biscuit with an olive sitting on top of it. Funny about that. Stewy doubled back and after a few grunts and groans he managed to pull me out. I grabbed the esky and we forged on to the nest, me feeling slightly rattled and covered in shit.

I started the slow process of getting the eggs out and then I heard a sound like someone blowing bubbles in the water. I spun around and there was a croc, no more than about 4 or 5 metres away. It must have been lying doggo in what looked like a shallow pool of muddy water but now it had decided that enough was enough and looked like it was getting ready to do some serious chomping. Stewy went to belt it in the snout, but the croc exploded out of the water, grabbed the paddle, shredded the end of it and flung it out of Stewy's hands. It went flying into the long grass. This took about half a second. The power and speed of the croc was unbelievable. Stewy backed up, turned to me and yelled, 'Mudgenna, mudgenna!' which is Aboriginal for 'Let's split the scene pronto'. We left in a hurry, making sure we avoided the muddy spot, as it wasn't a good time to get stuck.

The croc held its ground, jaws wide open, letting out an evil hissing sound. We regrouped, found the 14-foot paddle, which was now a 12-and-a-half-foot paddle with a frayed end, and headed back into the fight. We had no choice. The esky was still there next to the nest and we'd only got half of the eggs out. Stewy was mumbling, 'Yaka myanmuk,' which means, 'It's getting very hot in the bloody kitchen'. To his credit, Stewy was solid as a rock and he never looked like folding.

Stewy got a good one in early, which stunned the croc, but once again she got hold of the paddle, this time rolling her body and flinging the solid wooden oar into the long grass again. She then flew straight for us, jaws gaping wide open.

Stewy came out of the blocks looking like Jesse Owens set to break the Olympic long jump record in Berlin in 1936 and I wasn't far behind. Conservation Commission data sheets flying everywhere, I just had time to tick 'YES, THE FEMALE WAS PRESENT' and grab the esky. Off we went, flying through the long grass with the croc hot on the chase, but luckily for us she stopped once we were clear of the nest area. We agreed that round two had gone to the croc. We found the wooden oar, which now had been reduced to an 11-footer and was newly splintered at one end, and headed back to the chopper.

Phil taking the temperature of the nest with Stewy standing guard.

This was pretty well how it was for the next week. Flying, landing, mud, bush, crocs exploding out of all sorts of places, running, flying, landing, crocs lunging — moments of spectacular scenery and moments of sheer terror.

I wouldn't have missed it, no way. But by the end of a solid week of it, I felt like I'd just returned from a stint on the Kokoda Trail. The 14-foot paddle was down to 6 foot and showing signs of cracking. We'd collected about a thousand eggs and had them incubating away at the croc farm. Not quite the two thousand we'd hoped for, but a pretty good effort, and no one had been injured and me, Mick and Stewy had bonded together well.

The word came down the line: 'Meeting under the banyan tree at lunchtime.' We thought we were probably going to get a pat on the back or a medal or something, and we marched down as if it was an Anzac Day parade.

We proudly arrived at the banyan tree ready for all the accolades, but we couldn't have been more wrong. Someone had come up with the terrific idea of going out again for more eggs, this time to a place called Arafura Swamp.

Now Arafura Swamp is over towards central Arnhem Land. You couldn't find a more out-of-the-way place if you sat down and dedicated your life to it. Mick Dundee, who reckoned he knew the area, piped up and said, 'Great lizard country, bloody good lizard country.' And I didn't think he was talking about geckos! From what he was saying, the terrain would be a lot tougher and even more dangerous than what we'd already been through, the main reason being the abundance of what they call elephant grass. It grows around billabongs and waterways and is so high and thick you can lean on it. It can support a bloke's weight without even bending. You can imagine trying to hike through that shit.

I felt like I'd just done two tours of duty in Vietnam and now they were asking me to do another one. But sure enough, my lips formed those syllables: 'No worries, I'll have a go at that.' So off we went.

Two days later we were choppering into Arafura Swamp with a new 14-foot wooden oar strapped to the skid of the helicopter. Mick thought a big of insurance was in order and had got hold of an old revolver which looked like he'd borrowed it from John Wayne. It was shoved under the seat next to the Arnott's Family Assortment. Spirits were high as we came in low over the paperbarks — if I'd thought the Peter John flood plain was pretty, this place was absolutely exquisite. There was such an abundance of water birds that I thought at least the crocs would be well fed!

We started scanning the area looking for a nest. We didn't have to go far — there it was, a classic croc nest right on the edge of a bit of swamp surrounded by elephant grass, heaps of it. Mick landed about 150 metres from the nest, unfortunately as close as he could get. He decided to come with us this time and donned a Panama hat, looking very Jungle Jim. Stewy armed himself with the wooden paddle and we headed off.

The going was slow and hard, as we'd figured. It was so dense that Stewy had to rest the paddle on the grass, walk up it a metre or so and then repeat the process. We would have been roughly halfway to the nest with maybe another 50 or 60 metres to go, when all of a sudden the elephant grass up ahead was crashing down as if something was charging through it. Something big and coming our way. Crash, crash, bang, crash, crash, whoosh — it all happened so quickly. None of us had time to say or do anything. Before we knew it, the grass had parted directly in front of us and out came the wildest, ugliest, blackest, outright meanest-looking croc I'd ever seen, and it was right on us.

Stewy tried to reverse up, but backed into me and I went flying back into Mick. We all went arse up in a domino effect. We hit the deck, legs and arms going everywhere, like the Three Stooges doing a bit of slapstick. The croc could have grabbed any one of us. It was so close I could smell its breath. It had black weed hanging off its head and a full set of black slimy teeth and it was pissed off. It was there to do some bone-crushing.

Flying towards Arafura Swamp.

Mick was the only one who showed any real initiative. He was up and out of there. He hit the elephant grass so hard, I swear I could see the imprint of his body — just like in the cartoons when someone goes through a wall. He powered through the bush like the Six Million Dollar Man after a tune-up. Me and Stewy should have been with him, but we were still on the ground virtually nose to nose with the croc, not exactly sure which way we should play it, the croc sizing us up. We slowly backed away and got out of there.

We regrouped back at the chopper, a little rattled. We agreed to try Plan B, which was to scare it off with the helicopter. So we took off and Mick tried to buzz it with the chopper. The croc was lunging up and snapping, totally undaunted by the size and noise of the helicopter which just seemed to make it more annoyed.

Plan B wasn't getting us anywhere, so we landed. It looked like we'd have to try Plan C, which was to grab the John Wayne Memorial revolver from under the seat and head back in. Plan C didn't go over that well with Stewy. He was all for Plan D, which was to piss off and go somewhere else, preferably back home. But in true Aussie fighting tradition we marched back in. We had no intention of killing the croc, but at least we might be able to scare it. Maybe give it one around the tail or something, just to get it out the way so we could get to the nest.

Into the grass we went. It was easier this time as we'd already knocked a bit of a track down the first time. We got to the site of the previous ambush and there was no sign of the monster, so we picked up the paddle and the stuff that we'd left there and pushed on. We took the trail that the croc had made, working our way along it, our senses going overtime, expecting that at any moment the shit would hit the fan again.

We pushed on bit by bit, no talking. This was no joke. Everyone was concentrating, crouching low, pushing through the grass. The trail ended and we found ourselves at the nest. No croc.

Then about 20 metres away, a grotesque, weed-ridden head came up out of the water, let out a guttural groan and started swimming towards us. Stewy mumbled something that sounded like 'Yo narma', which means roughly, 'Hasta la vista, baby'. Then he opened up with the John Wayne Memorial and to my surprise, the antique actually worked. He fired a few shots around her head to try and frighten her off. We seemed to have her bluffed. She stayed in the water just groaning her head off, and Mick and I got the eggs out as quickly as we could.

Just as we thought things were sweet, the croc made another charge through the water. Stewy lined the gun up and pulled the trigger . . . nothing — we were out of bullets. So we grabbed the gear and we floated. This time it was us crashing through the elephant grass — and we didn't look back until we reached the chopper!

This little drama set the precedent for Arafura Swamp. There were plenty more escapades and narrow escapes, stand-offs and take-offs, but somehow we got through it. Stewy and Mick were good blokes to work with, and I think it brought out the best in all of us.

We got our quota of two thousand eggs for the farm but we sure did it the hard way. Then again, I don't think there really is an easy way to collect croc eggs!

They Just Don't Make 'Em Like That Anymore

I first met Ron when I started working for a safari tour mob in Darwin. This particular company handled mainly overseas tourists and offered a range of camping tours to places such as Kakadu National Park. Ronny was the best and most experienced guide they had, so since I was the new boy the company figured it would be a good idea for me to tag along with Ron on one of his tours to get orientated and pick up a few tips from the master.

Ron had one of the most colourful histories of anyone I'd ever met. As a young bloke he served in the British Navy in World War Two before coming out to Australia. It didn't take long before Ron found himself taking to the Australian bush as if he'd been born and bred for it. He became a stockman, and later on a drover of some repute, before a twist of fate found him fighting in the Korean War.

Actually it wasn't really a twist of fate. Being a bit of a lad in his younger days Ron once rode his horse into a pub in Katherine for a laugh. Once inside the pub, the horse decided to go mad and proceeded to kick the living shit out of everything inside. This included tables, chairs, mirrors, bottles, doors, windows and a few people! And in true Territory tradition Ron never shifted from the saddle. The Katherine police fronted up and there was a slight altercation and a few knockouts, and Ronny was having the time of his life, but for some reason the local constabulary didn't quite take it too well. They presented Ronny with two options.

'It's like this, Ron — the Army's looking for blokes to go to Korea, and Fanny Bay Gaol is looking for blokes as well. What's it gunna be?'

Ron opted for Korea and found himself in another war. It was no picnic and he saw a lot of things he'd rather forget. On his return to Australia the bush embraced him once again and over the years Ron created a name for himself in outback Australia.

He was tough and he was hard, but always quick with a joke and a laugh. He possessed the staunch principles and manners of a generation of fair dinkum Australians that evolved from a tough, honest part of our history. The clichéd phrase 'They don't make 'em like that any more' has never rung so true. Ron always took things as they came. As far as he was concerned you were innocent till proven guilty and he'd give anyone a fair go. But if crossed, Ronny could really deal it out. One old mate of mine reckoned the only way to stop Ron when he was in full flight would be to cut off his head. Fortunately Ronny took a lot of provoking to really crank up.

In the seventies, when the Top End flood plains were full of water buffalo, Ron got hold of a fair piece of country and built himself a meatworks, and for years was a big player in the buffalo industry, exporting buff meat around Australia and then overseas. Ron would spend many a day hunting buffalo out on the flood plains, and with a hundred bullets he could drop a hundred and one buffalo, that's providing the last two were standing close together. But the era of the buffalo came and went in the Northern Territory, and Ronny decided it was time to take on the biggest, the most dangerous and the most nerve-racking challenge of his life. No, not hunting crocodiles or buffalo; no, not breaking in wild horses or fighting in wars; no, something even more terrifying. You guessed it — dealing with the general public! Ronny became a tour guide.

Now Ron knew every bird, billabong, hill, tree, and every Aboriginal rock painting and green ant nest in the Top End. He was missing a few teeth and a few fingers but he was still a warrior and a genuine slice of the outback and people loved to be around him. In his blue singlet and caved-in old hat, Ronny would hike mile after mile up and down through the rugged splendour of Kakadu, and if you were good enough to keep up Ron would show you the world. If you weren't, he'd simply pick you up on the way back. For a bloke his age he was extremely fit and no one loved the bush more than he did.

As far as the tourists were concerned he could pretty well do no wrong. When it was dinnertime Ronny would just throw a few chops on a plate and say, 'If you want a chop, cook it.' They loved his rugged attitude. If Ron had got them up at four in the morning and told them to go and sit on an ants' nest, they'd have done it. And they'd still say what a great bloke he was! Ron had 'em on a string.

So Ron and me teamed up. Ronny was the Legend and I was his offsider.

One Sunday morning about six o'clock there we were, fumbling around in the half-dark trying to get the gear ready for a four-day camping safari in Kakadu. We were running late and we had ten American tourists to pick up. Me being young and keen, I'm starting to panic and I look across at Ron and say, 'Shit, we're gunna be late, Ron.' Ron looked up, slowly took a bite from his apple and matter-of-factly said, 'Well, fuck 'em.' Ron was not only a settling influence, he was a man who got straight to the point.

We eventually rounded everyone up from their respective motels and headed off, Kakadu-bound. It wasn't a bad group — a few of your cigar-smoking office types, a young couple, an older couple and a lovely middle-aged lady who was a psychologist.

Ronny blasted through the outer suburbs of Darwin rattling off a few statistics, with everyone very excited. Once we were clear of civilisation we stopped a few times and Ron pointed out various things of interest. Then we called into the old Bark Hut Inn for smoko. Over coffee, Ron gave me a little piece of advice. He said I was being too nice to everyone. He pointed out that if you start off a tour too nice, everyone expects you to be nice the whole trip. He said, 'You should be like me — I start off a grumpy old prick, and anything after that's a bonus for 'em.'

So off we went rattling around Kakadu. The first day went really well — some great scenery and a look at some age-old rock art — and in the cool of the afternoon we set up camp. Ronny sizzled up a few chops and told some yarns and the group loved him. I think as far as they were concerned Ron was the genuine Crocodile Dundee and I reckon they weren't far off.

That night the mozzies came in fierce, as they often do in that part of the country, and they ripped into everyone. In the morning we were all a bit jaded — all except Ron of course. He had skin like riding-boot leather and never felt a thing. So he was as chirpy as hell after eight hours of sleep and it was all go. There just weren't enough hours in the day for a bloke like Ron — waterfalls to see, billabongs to swim in — and later that day he decided we'd do a 6-kilometre hike straight uphill to see if the group was fit enough to handle the 12-kilometre hike he had planned for the next day.

Ron found the hill he had in mind and then it was onwards and upwards. One of the cigar-smoking Americans asked, 'Rarny . . . Rarny . . . why do we have to climb this damn hill, Rarny?'

Ron spun around, clenched his fists and said, 'Cause it's here,' and off he went. His legs were in four-wheel drive and he wasn't looking back.

Once on top, although the group were near collapse, the rewards were great. The views were spectacular and to see the Aboriginal rock art that Ron knew was up there was well worth the effort.

For a bloke in his sixties Ron had the constitution of a Brahman bull and he could go all day. Unfortunately the same couldn't be said about the group or me, and by the time we got back to camp we were well and truly stuffed.

But the sun wasn't quite down yet and Ronny said, 'Why don't we have a bit of a cool-off down at the billabong?'

Everyone reckoned it was a great idea, so we grabbed our towels and headed off down the track leading to the waterhole. It wasn't far and in we went and it was beautiful, washing the sweat off, enjoying the crystal clear water, everyone relaxing . . . Well everyone except Ronny and the charming American psychologist, Kathleen. They'd disappeared over a hill.

I started doing a bit of thinking and it all started to add up. Earlier that day I'd noticed that every time Kathleen came near Ron he'd start spinning off the botanical name of every living thing in a 10-kilometre radius, just trying to sugar her up a bit. And I think it had worked. Kathleen was obviously taken with him — it was either that or Ronny's got her over the hill to show her a couple of frogs or some bush tucker or something. Anyway, it wasn't any of my business.

As the sun slowly disappeared and the lights went out on the escarpment country of Kakadu, we meandered back to camp. Soon after, Kathleen and Ronny turned up, Kathleen with a grin from ear to ear and Ron looking sheepish, and I'm thinking, people don't glow like that after checking out a few frogs. Ron had transformed himself from the rugged outdoor type to the Sheik from Scrubby Creek and he was sweeping her off her feet, nothing surer. Later that night I noticed Kathleen drag her swag up close to Ronny's and I'm thinking, either Ron's pointing out the Southern Cross or else they're really enjoying each other's company.

The next morning Ron was up at sparrow fart galloping around the camp like a young horse on oats, his top lip curled right back. He was keen to get out there. If there was one thing he hated it was burning good daylight.

So after a quick breakfast of chops à la Ronny, we hit the trail. This was the big day because we were exploring the gorge country of southern Kakadu — Ron's favourite area. And as the day unfolded I could see why. It was one glorious panorama after the next. We swam, we climbed and we staggered through mile after mile of fantastic, rugged Kakadu, Ronny power-walking out in front and the rest of us wandering behind in various stages of exhaustion.

It was like a scene from the Burma Railway, but somehow Ron had taken us through the pain barrier. We all saw so much and learnt so much, and with every botanical name that Ronny rattled off, Kathleen would just melt.

That night back at camp, spirits were really high, everyone nursing blisters and tending sunburn after the big day. Ron slam-dunked a few chops and we all talked about what a great adventure we'd had.

Ron was not only a settling influence, he was a man who got straight to the point.

'You see,' Ronny pointed out, 'there's two ways you can attack a tour. You can go drink coffee and sit around visitors' centres looking at displays all day, or else you can get out there and really feel the country and get something out of it.'

Although everyone was totally rooted, the group was unanimous it had been a time they'd never forget — the trip of a lifetime.

The old swag called and I was happy to lay my bones down that night. Ron and Kathleen had joined their swags together to form a type of cocoon, and as it was the last night I think Ronny wanted to make sure Kathleen knew where the Southern Cross was.

Next day we rolled back into Darwin, everyone a little melancholy that the whole thing was coming to an end. Ron was going to 'style up' big time and shout Kathleen a pizza, and after I'd dropped everyone off at their motels I was heading out to find a book on the botanical names of plants. It obviously worked for Ron because Kathleen moved to the Northern Territory and married him.

For me, working with Ron had been a real experience and I'd made a really good mate. And as far as I know, Ronny's still walking around out there somewhere, discovering country people never even knew existed. As I said, they just don't make 'em like that anymore.

Holy Mackerel

The SOS came in the form of a phone call. On the other end of the line was the stressed-out voice of an old mate of mine, Steve Norman, mackerel fisherman. He was really under the pump. Things were tight financially and the only light at the end of the tunnel was to fill up with fish when the mackerel season started. He needed a good deckhand. I'm always the bloke they ring when there's a job no one else wants to do. But what could I say? He was a mate and he needed help. I hadn't had much to do with the sea before so I thought, what the hell, catch a few fish, have a look around . . . Yeah, count me in.

Steve was no ordinary mackerel fisherman. He had a relationship with the sea that went deeper than most. It was a spiritual thing with Steve. The sea was a living, breathing entity. It had a voice, and thoughts, and moods. But above all, in control of the whole show, was THE SEA GOD. Now this might sound far-fetched, but you have to take into account that people who live and work all their lives at sea form certain views.

So Steve used to sit on the bow of his boat, go into a trance, chew the fat with the Sea God and, with any luck, get the good oil on where the fish were biting. I knew all

Steve's main boat, Imagine.

this because another good mate of mine, Mark Johnson, had worked for Steve a bit and he'd filled me in. Mark had taken off to Indonesia, which was how I ended up being roped in. Steve was a good operator, Mark reckoned, tough, safety-conscious, good-humoured, reliable, and he had the added bonus of those visions of where the fish were biting. What more could you ask for from a skipper?

In the north of Australia the strong winds of the dry season ease off around September and that's when Steve usually headed out to sea in search of mackerel, his bread and butter. But not the year I helped him. Steve had heard the winds were going to drop off early this year. I'm not sure where he heard that — via the Sea God or someone at the Yacht Club bar — but as we steamed out in early August, waves breaking over the front of the boat, I'm thinking, if this is the wind when it's dropped off, I'd hate to be around when it cranks up.

I went green just as we passed the jetty. It was rough and getting rougher, but this was the good bit. About six hours later it was really rough, even for Steve, so we detoured in behind a pretty island called Truant and sheltered in a lovely horseshoe-shaped bay. The place was full of dolphins, obviously hiding out there as well. You know it's really rough when actual sea creatures don't go out in it.

Steve thought it was a good time to put me through some training before things got serious. Mackerel fishing, he pointed out, was gentlemen's fishing, nothing too high-tech. It was an old-style way of fishing and over the years hasn't changed much. Towed behind the main boat were two smaller craft, little dinghies called dories, and you each head off in one of these and trawl a couple of lines out the back with lures attached. When you hook up a mackerel you 'patch up', which means going around in circles trying to pull in as many macks as possible. In theory it all seemed great, and in the sheltered waters of Truant Island it was fine, wheeling around in the little dory, going through the motions, with Steve yelling instructions from the other dory.

There were no macks in the bay. That would have been too easy. So we just poked around for the next few days in the bay, did some maintenance on the boat, rigged up fishing lines, and I worked on my dory-handling skills. Truant was a fascinating island. Turtles nested on the beaches at night in their droves, and there seemed to be evidence of goats on the island. The story was that back in the old Captain Cook days, they dropped a few goats off on the islands here and there, so they'd have a few chops on tap next time they were in the area. There was the wreck of a trawler on one reefy point on the island — I don't know the story there. There were birds and gulls of all kinds and there were the dolphins. They'd obviously come to the conclusion that they weren't going anywhere in this weather, and throughout the day gangs of them would swim up to Steve's boat and have a good old look at what the humans were up to. Or maybe Steve communicated with them, who knows?

One sunset Steve sat on the bow, reclined back into his tartan deck chair, let his eyes roll back and tranced out. I watched the whole thing from the wheelhouse. Steve went deeper and deeper, letting out the odd mumble and even twitching a bit. I'd say at a rough guess he was getting some vibes. Whether he'd got through to the Sea God, I couldn't tell. For all I knew he was out with the dolphins. But I figured that being a dedicated mackerel fisherman, it wouldn't be long before Steve would forget about the weather and start chasing fish around. And I was right.

The sea was in his blood, it was ingrown in his toe-nails, the sea was his church. Steve was just another living organism on the ocean, he was part of its ecology, and when he dies his parting wish will no doubt be to be filleted and boxed and placed in the chiller with his beloved mackerel.

'Early start,' Steve said. 'We're gonna steam to the top of the Wessel Islands, get amongst them. Wind will be dropping off.'

So next morning we're up and we're gone. It was early and the sea hadn't had time to turn blue, it was still that gunmetal grey colour of the pre-dawn. I took one look back at the bay and the dolphins — they weren't going anywhere. They knew better. The sea was violent all day, huge waves coming from all directions. It was as though we were in a giant washing machine, Steve's boat pitching and rolling, the two dories bobbing around bravely in the whitewash behind. It was a humbling experience, eating dry crackers and spewing my guts out every second wave.

By the time we reached the top of the Wessels, I felt like I'd just done a twelve-hour shift on a mechanical bull in top gear. My stomach didn't know if it was coming or going. Mostly going, but I made sure not to whinge or show any signs of faltering to Steve, because this is what fishing is all about. These are the conditions and I was getting paid so I tried to just do my duty, thinking all these huge seas were the norm.

We anchored in a bay out of the extreme weather, although the wind would have still blown a dog off its chain. The sea was a little calmer though, which gave my stomach a reprieve. Steve vibed on to the Sea God in the deck chair on the bow and I prepared a few lines for the morning. It looked like we were going to give it a go.

Four o'clock came around quickly and I woke in my swag on the deck, wind cutting into me and nearly blowing the clothes off the make-shift clothes line on the bow. Steve was chafing at the bit. Kettle on, dories fuelled up, he was wired, as though he'd just been electrocuted by the toaster and survived. After a cup of coffee strong enough to put hair on the chest of a coral trout, we saddled up and, after some last-minute instructions from Steve, who assured me he wouldn't be far away, we chugged off in our respective dories into a raging black wilderness.

Now I've had some nerve-racking jobs. I've caught crocodiles, mixed it up with crazy horses, had a gun pointed at me, but, mate, you can multiply all that by ten and you still wouldn't come near the fear involved in that mackerel fishing trip. We left the relative shelter of the bay and I immediately started to get buffeted by a wild sea, waves smashing into the dory from all sides. And as it was still dark, I couldn't even see Steve, who despite assuring me he would stay close, disappeared straightaway. I found myself bobbing around like a cork and I honestly thought I'd be putting the cue in the rack and wouldn't be seeing smoko. This was it. I'd be hanging my shirts in Davey Jones's locker before I knew it.

First light started to glow on the horizon and I suddenly remembered why I was actually out there in the first place, and threw my two lines over. Catching mackerel was definitely the last thing on my mind — staying alive was taking pride of place. I tried to keep the dory's nose front-on into the biggest waves. If I copped one side-on, it would have capsized the dory without even trying. As the sun came up, I caught a glimpse of Steve spearing down the face of a huge wave out in the distance. It was like a surfing version of 'The Man from Snowy River'. Then I lost him again.

Then bang! One of my lines went stiff. So, like the well-trained fisherman I was, I sent the dory into a circle and patched up, getting smashed by waves and trying to pull the fish in, and this thing was fighting. I finally got it up to the dory and lifted it in. It was a Big Mack all right and, like I'd been taught, I grabbed the club and went to belt it on the scone. Waves were coming over the dory and I tried to concentrate. I swung the club and the bloody thing slipped out of my hand and went into the water. Before I even had time to reach over and grab the club, a shark came up from nowhere and fucking ate it!

You could have knocked me over with a mozzie coil. This put a completely new perspective on mackerel fishing. If a shark just ate the club, what the hell was going to happen if I went in the drink? I went into shock thinking I could be part of the food chain at any minute. All of a sudden Steve emerged out of a wave, yelled, 'Get back to the boat, it's too rough,' and revved off. That was the best news I'd had for a while, so back to the boat I slogged.

Steve had caught a few and I had my unclubbed 50-pounder. So we set about filleting them and within no time at all a great collection of sharks, giant cod, trevally and even school of garfish had formed up at the back of the boat, competing for the skeletons and off-cuts being discarded into the water. There was serious hunting and gathering going on at the back of the boat, with trevally

Sharks hanging around the boat.

being bitten in two by sharks and cod the size of 44-gallon drums giving as good as they got from the sharks. It was a frenzy. The garfish were even having a go, but suffering huge casualties. For anyone who believes in reincarnation, I'll give you the big tip: whatever you do, don't come back as a garfish.

Later that day, after Steve's special coffee, so strong it would put fire in the belly of a Himalayan snow leopard, we saddled up once again and chugged off in the dories. The one good thing about fishing in the afternoon as opposed to the morning is the fact you can actually see where you are going. But now, knowing what lurked within the depths, constipation was never going to be an issue on this trip.

The next week saw us venture out occasionally, but it was just too rough and we'd come chugging back again. This frustrated Steve, for he was born to catch mackerel, and not only that, he had to fill his 3-ton freezer with fillets to cash up. The coffees got stronger, the silences got longer, and the ecosystem at the back of the boat waited patiently. This was the life of a fisherman, an honest, simple life. In between near-death experiences, you drank coffee, read *Playboy* and waited.

Steve sat out on the bow again one day in the tartan deck chair and must have cracked the right frequency because the wind dropped. It didn't drop much, but enough to give us a go. Next morning, after a cuppa that made my hair spike straight up like the quills of an echidna, we headed out and took up the challenge. The sea was still rough and life-threatening and terrifying, but not quite as bad as it had previously been. This time we made it out a bit further and there were plenty of mackerel around, also plenty of sharks — hammerheads, tigers, you name it. They were coming in from everywhere. They'd obviously worked out that it was easier to grab a mackerel once I'd already hooked it, because with every fish I caught it was a battle. Often I just pulled in a head minus the body, and it wasn't uncommon to see a mackerel launch itself out of the water with a shark, totally airborne, right up its backside. It was an awesome display. I even had sharks attacking the outboard on the dory, but as time went on I got quicker and started to beat the sharks a bit, though not all the time.

Every now and again I'd get a glimpse of Steve shooting along the horizon, at one with the dory, Clancy of the Overflow wheeling the lead of a mob of brumby mackerel. Born and bred to the sea, Steve was great to watch. He'd club the fish, cut its throat and with a flick of the wrist have the lure back in the water ready to go again.

So the routine evolved: catch fish, go back to the boat, fillet, clean, rest, coffee, catch, go back to the boat, fillet, etc. There was plenty of mack action, shark action and bowel action.

After nearly a month, my nervous system was like shredded cabbage but I was still managing to function. Steve never said too much but we were putting a few fillets away and that was the main thing. One morning, after downing possibly the strongest coffee known to mankind, we set out into the black jungle of roaring swell at pre-dawn. As usual Steve disappeared straight off and I threw my two lines out praying to God to let me survive another day.

Steve in action, filleting a big mackerel.

The wind had picked up and it was looking serious again. As first light shared itself with us ocean dwellers, I could see I'd accidentally drifted in a bit close to a fairly shallow reef area. Steve had warned me several times not to get anywhere near this area as the swell sucks right up there and then just dumps, so the water would go from under the dory and I'd be smashed by the overfalls. I was still a way off, but it was something to watch.

Then bang! My line went off, some huge mackerel no doubt, and it jerked my dory around. As I went to pull it in, it took off and the last thing I wanted to happen happened. The line got tangled around the prop and stalled the motor. It all happened quickly. The mackerel was going crazy on the end of the line, which was wrapped good and proper around the propeller. I looked around and saw that the white water from Steve's killer reef was looming and the current was taking me straight for it, and fast. I couldn't believe it, but that's the sea for you. Things happen quickly, and if you're not sharp enough it's the food chain, no questions asked.

Steve appeared out of nowhere like a torpedo and yelled, 'Get out your anchor or you're dead,' then disappeared into a wave. I dived for the hatch that held the anchor — it had fourteen wing nuts holding it shut. Nothing like trying to undo fourteen wing nuts with about forty-five seconds left on the clock before you get smashed on a reef and then torn apart by sharks! Steve shot past again, but I didn't hear what he was yelling, I was too focused on the wing nuts. With about one second up my sleeve I got the anchor out and it pulled me up just short of the overfalls crashing down on the reef. Fair dinkum, it was one of the closest calls I'd ever had. For a moment there I thought my time on the planet had run out.

Steve was in the horrors, yelling out all sorts of instructions, roaring up and down in his dory, the poor bloke. He knew the dangers only too well. If something had happened to me, I was replaceable, but no way could Steve afford a new dory. I cut the line free from the outboard, pulled up the anchor and got out of there.

But that was it for me, I'd run my race. That little episode shook me up and I was hanging up the hand-line! In these conditions I was on borrowed time. So when we fought the swell and got back to the boat, I laid my cards on the table. I told Steve straight out, 'That's it. I'm not goin' out there again, wild horses couldn't drag me.'

I expected a blast of 'Don't be so weak, this is what fishing is all about' and braced myself, ready for Steve's verbal spray. But Steve said, 'Yeah, mate, fair enough. If you're not goin' out there, I'm not either. Been shittin' meself the whole time, never worked in anything this bad before.'

You could have knocked me over with a piece of paper bark. I'll be buggered, I thought. I'd spent one whole month of thinking I was going to die at least twice a day in conditions that I thought were the norm for fishing!

Well, anyway, we sat out on the bow, had a laugh and a coffee Steve had whipped up, and chewed the fat. Steve had taken chances because of his financial situation, otherwise he wouldn't have left the yacht club bar in this weather. I was wishing we'd had this conversation a month ago.

Anyway, Steve made enough out of the fish we'd caught to get himself going again, and I headed bush, vowing never to go anywhere near the sea ever again, not even a fish and chip shop. Still, that month couldn't really be described as an adventure that got me nowhere, because I'd learnt quite a bit from old Steve, and it was good to see a bloke like him in action. He was a real master mariner, no doubt about it.

Later that same year Steve nearly came unstuck himself. Fishing back up the Wessels, a shark stuck its head straight up through the floor of Steve's dory. Apparently it was charging after a mackerel, miscalculated and rammed the bottom of the wooden dory, coming right through the floor. Luckily Steve's new offsider got over there quickly and rescued Steve before the dory sank. When Steve got

Phil O'Brien, master of the waves,
holding a big mackerel.

back to the main boat he sat down and smoked a whole packet of Winfield Red, one after the other, and ate coffee straight out the tin.

So if you're looking for a little adventure, try something relaxing like catching crocs or politics. Unless you've got nothing at all to live for, don't even think about mackerel fishing!

The Croc Attack

When a bloke lives in the Northern Territory and writes a book, it's almost compulsory to devote at least one chapter to a croc attack, or a near croc attack. I mean, a book coming out of the Territory just wouldn't be valid without a croc attack in it. People would say, 'Oh yeah, it's not a bad book, but where's the croc attack?' And the critics would tear shreds off it: 'No substance, no croc attack, this book doesn't measure up . . .'

In Darwin, if a croc attack hasn't featured in the front-page headlines for the month, people ask why. A huge croc caught in Darwin Harbour's great — it's front page every time. Or an attendant gets mauled — good stuff. Even a hatchling popping up in a stormwater drain usually gets a headline. The croc attack is an important part of society in the Top End. The economy booms after every attack, the media sells papers, the pubs are full of blokes who reckon they were there, and film crews come in their droves to try and video the next one. Any local worth their salt has been attacked at least once or twice, and many an appendix scar has been revealed to the tune of 'the bastard really had me'. So as an author and citizen of the Top End I feel obliged to share my own very humble croc attack.

I'd been camped all week at the most beautiful place a bloke could ever imagine: crystal-clear turquoise water, white sand, sunrises and sunsets I can't even begin to describe. Sea eagles gliding overhead, schools of mullet moving like shadows up and down the shallows, manta rays launching high out of the water — it was as if I was living in a David Attenborough documentary. The north-east Territory coast is a pristine area, and to this day I haven't found any place I like better Looking out to sea from under the shade of a casuarina, it never occurred to me something out there actually wanted to eat me. The place was just so welcoming and beautiful I couldn't help but relax and let the old guard down.

I'd been employed by the Northern Territory University in Darwin to set up a camp on the beach so that a team of scientists could base themselves there for a month or so to study sea turtles. They were planning to tag them and place satellite-tracking devices on their shells to find out more about their habits and where they travel. It was all interesting stuff and I was excited to be part of the project — even though I was the brawn and they were the brains, my role was still an important one. I had to provide a generator for power, a supply of water, lighting, fuel, food and even a long-drop, but the place was spectacular and it was no chore at all working there.

I'd arrived a good week before the university mob, just to get everything squared away. There was a small shack there which had been home to an Aboriginal family who had moved up the coast a bit — it would make a handy headquarters for the turtle crew. So there I was, lying back one evening, enjoying the remoteness and the solitude, strumming my guitar at my camp up the beach a bit. With the high tide lapping at my feet, it was paradise.

I was two-thirds through a cask of rough red, singing 'Take Me Home Country Road' to whichever coastal sea creatures that wanted to listen. Not a care in the world, a balmy sea breeze caressing its way through the casuarina tree, the gentle lapping of the water, the chatter of flying foxes, and me singing badly on a dark but starry night. Then, don't ask me why, a gut feeling, a sixth-sense sort of feeling, came over me. So I stopped strumming, picked up my torch, switched it on and shone it at the water's edge at my feet.

Nothing. Just the gentle ripples of the tide washing in. But it just goes to show you should never ignore a genuine gut feeling, because I strummed the guitar about twice and then went for the torch again, and there, right at the water's edge, just in front of me, was a bloody big croc with its head up out of the water and mouth wide open, poised to move forward.

I don't know what made me grab the torch the second time, but if I hadn't I'm sure that croc would have nailed me. I reckon it had been lying just under the water out of view, creeping up bit by bit, and I caught it just before it made the final lunge.

Once I shone the torch on it the croc knew it had been sprung. It turned its head slowly to the side and with one eye looked right through me for a moment, then it slowly backed away and disappeared.

If not for that sixth sense, which I didn't even know I had, I could have been a headline. These days I've learnt to trust that gut feeling and it's fair dinkum got me through some scrapes. But back to the beach . . . Crocs are sneaky, calculating creatures and you've got to be one step ahead of them. So I thought I was pretty smart moving camp into the old shack later that night. This'll be safe, I'm thinking. How wrong I was.

All the sixth sense in the world couldn't have predicted what happened that night. A family of quolls ran across my swag all night, chewing my hair and fighting and hissing at one another. They tore all my bread to pieces, gnawed at every piece of fruit I had and managed to shit everywhere. A quoll is like a possum with attitude and a lot more teeth.

So what started as a genuinely euphoric night strumming my guitar in paradise, was disturbed by a close encounter with a big lizard, and then to top it off a bloke finally gets shat on all night by quolls and I tell you what . . . there's no glory in that.

I know this will devastate and disillusion a lot of Top End residents, but I'll be taking my chances with the crocs in the future because, mate, it's the quolls you've really got to worry about.

You Can't Hide in a Glasshouse

The wet season in the Top End stretches from roughly Christmas to Easter, and because of the heavy falls of rain things out bush go a bit quiet round that time. Roads get washed out, creeks and rivers rise. It's really no time to be travelling around, and because of the conditions it can be hard to find work at that time of the year.

The idea is to save up during the dry and then sit out the wet, but when you're like me, a totally unorganised, irresponsible, financial disaster, the wet season can be a pretty lean time. I've had the seats out of the car looking for loose change on more than one occasion.

Life's a fickle thing, more ins and outs than a blue movie. One day you've got cream in your coffee and next day you're resoaking your old tea-bags. So the go is, you've got to grab the opportunities that come your way, hold on tight, be responsible and plan for the future. The perfect example of my inability to do this is the time I got offered a job at a prestigious national park. It was only for the wet season because some bloke was on long-service leave, but it could lead to a full-time position, they reckoned. I jumped at it.

It paid well, the conditions were great, there was a chance of advancement *and* I got to wear this real deadly National Parks and Wildlife uniform with badges and logos hanging off it everywhere. There was a career here for the taking, a chance to put my past behind me and become a responsible citizen, maybe even get a tax-file number. This was my one big break and I was going to hold on tight. No way was I going to stuff this one up as I'd done so many times before with other jobs. This was different, I was in for the long haul!

They started me off at what they called the Entry Station, a flash new structure with stylish glass walls. As the tourists drove into the park, they had to pull up at the Entry Station. I'd take their entry fees, give them maps and help them plan their trip. As I was the first person they saw when they came into the park, it was important to present myself well, the park being a World Heritage area. The tourists, mainly overseas visitors, expected a high standard of service, which I reckoned I could fake.

Things were going well. The Entry Station was really decked out, with air conditioning, a fridge, a microwave, a phone — it was paradise. I wasn't supposed to be sleeping there as well, but it was heaps more comfortable than the busted-arse caravan I was meant to be staying in. And after all, who was to know?

This was proving to be an all-time great wet season — meeting all sorts of tourists, making good money, wearing a rip-roaring uniform and soaking up some great air-con. I'd never had it so good . . . until I met these four Irish girls.

Their van pulled in at the Entry Station and they had 'good time' written all over their pretty Irish faces. I did the entry fee and the map thing and we started rapping away. They suggested I meet them down at their camp for a drink after work. I'm thinking, how much better can life get?

So after work I cruised down to their camp and slipped right into it. As with most Irish people I've met, they were very charming and a lot of fun. One drink led to about seventeen and the last thing I remember I was playing a penny whistle and doing an Irish jig around the fire. I think I finally headed back to the Entry Station about three or four in the morning, fully marinated.

Then horror struck.

The next morning I woke up to about thirty Germans banging on the glass walls of the Entry Station, and there's me, no clothes on at all, choked down on top of my swag. I must have slept though the alarm! There was no hiding because the joint was all glass. They had their faces pressed up against it, some of them had even started taking photos. In full view I somehow got my shorts on and went over and slid the door open. I was looking rough — no shirt, no shoes, staggering around like I had mad cow disease, penny whistles still playing in my brain. I was shot to pieces. I had a hangover that would have killed a Shetland pony. The Germans were probably wondering if they had the right address.

I took their money and threw a few maps around, but the Germans didn't know what the hell was going on. As the coach driver ushered them back on the bus I heard him say, 'Interesting wildlife around here, isn't it, folks.'

'Ja, ja,' they said.

Needless to say, my temporary position which was to turn into a full-time position had suddenly gone from temporary to 'Thanks for coming'.

I'd blown another one.

Drinks Waiter Blues

At last count I worked out I'd had about two hundred jobs and none of them had got me anywhere. But whichever way you looked at it, no one could say I hadn't tried. I sometimes think I try too hard. Like the time I thought I'd go south and check out Melbourne, broaden my horizons a bit.

In those days, I was ever the optimist, always on the lookout for that silver lining. All I needed was a break, a fair go. So it was my first day in Melbourne and I was walking down Bourke Street, taking it all in. There must have been ten thousand people rushing up and down and in and out of shops and buildings, and it was all fairly up-tempo. I meandered along at my usual pace and next minute two girls came up to me and said straight up, 'Would you like to have some fun?' I don't know why they picked me, but I said, 'Yeah', thinking they were just being friendly. Then they said, 'We've got a place around the corner — give us fifty bucks and we'll go and have a good time.' I can't say I thought too deeply about the whole thing — the natives were friendly and I always was a sucker for adventure. So thinking this could possibly broaden my horizons I found myself handing over fifty dollars.

Well, they pocketed my fifty ... and bolted! They took off so fast I'd say they covered the first hundred metres in record Olympic time, probably a personal best. The last thing I saw was the soles of their sandshoes disappearing down Bourke Street, and they were smoking. The other nine thousand nine hundred and ninety-nine people on Bourke Street didn't even blink an eyelid. A mate had told me that my money wouldn't last long in Melbourne — well, I never even got to spend the first fifty. I'd been done like a dinner.

So with my shoulders slumped and my spirit broken, I merged into the crowd, getting hip-and-shouldered out the way by businessmen in black suits and jostled along by a herd of Chinese university students surging towards McDonald's. I was feeling down, so after nearly being trampled by a group of Greeks leaving a coffee shop I decided to find a bar, sit down and take a good long hard look at myself. I was going nowhere in life and it was starting to be so obvious, that I was standing out in a crowd, as if I had 'loser' tattooed across my forehead. Those two girls hadn't had much trouble picking me out, that was for sure. So it was time for a beer and a bit of the old deep-and-meaningful to see if I could come up with a new angle on becoming a more respected member of society. It was time I tried to better myself.

So I ducked into a bar and, after nearly getting steamrollered by a mob of Lebanese on their way out after a business lunch, I dragged my low self-esteem up to the counter and ordered a beer. The Italian barman resembled a young Sylvester Stallone and had about a dozen women hanging off his every move. He wore pants so tight you could see what he'd had for breakfast, which at a rough guess was a fairly long bit of strasbourg. He was pretty cool, spinning glasses around and twirling bottles, flicking ice out the ice bucket, sending it way up in the air and then catching it in the glass behind his back. A little two-step, a pirouette, some chat with the chicks — this guy was on fire. His lunchtime audience were obviously regulars because they knew the routine. When young Sylvester leapt up on top of the bar with a bottle of tequila, the women snapped their heads back and opened their mouths. It reminded me of a documentary I saw once about when the mother bird flies back to the nest with some worms and stuff, and the young are waiting with gaping jaws, ready to devour whatever gets put down their throats. He spun the 750ml bottle, flicked the cap off and from a great height proceeded to pour the tequila straight down the gullet of the first girl, who fairly gulped into it. When she started to gag he moved on to the next keen participant, working his way along the lot of them. I even had a guzzle myself, and I'm thinking, what an operator. He was in full flight.

The girls were getting pretty chirpy after the big top-up and they all started crowing about some type of cocktail, which seemed to really excite the barman. He spun around, hopped up and down and gyrated all over the place, then formed up twelve shot glasses full of some weird-looking blue formula. Then he played his trump.

With blinding speed he hooked a bottle off the shelf and with a quick sweep splashed this stuff all around the shot glasses. In one fluid motion he lit it up with his cigarette lighter and blue flames leapt from the bar. The mob went wild and I'm thinking, what do they call this cocktail — Boil the Billy?

This guy had them in the palm of his hand and on his command the girls blew the fire out and skulled with gusto. You wouldn't have to be a Tibetan monk to work out this bloke wouldn't be going home to an empty swag. Not like me — I'd forked out fifty and still missed out. As I stared with envy at the barman his face seemed to melt away and like a special effect in a movie it was replaced with mine. For a dreamy couple of minutes I could see myself rapping away behind the bar, girls drooling with every shake of my cocktail shaker, me floating from girl to girl, organising which one was lucky enough to meet me after I knocked off work.

Let's face it, I was dreaming. But did it really have to be just a dream? First step: find a shop that sold tight black pants and bow ties, find a job, and start racking up some results. Just like the Italian Stallion. I was going to go from a loser to a winner — if he could do it, I could do it, no River Murrays.

Back on Bourke Street it was still all go, cappuccinos being demolished left right and centre and the Chinese university students were now schooling in front of Hoyts Cinema complex. No matter where you looked, it was action. I broke into a jog down Bourke Street, looking for a bow tie and some black strides, moving through the crowds like an unregistered dog. The future seemed bright, optimism surged through my veins.

That night, back at my budget accommodation on Little Collins Street, I felt pretty pleased with myself. I'd picked up the black pants for next to nothing. The bow tie had set me back a bit but it was an investment, I kept telling myself. Next day I was back on the streets looking for a job — the job that was going to transform me. As that fateful day wore on, keen as I was, finding a nice cushy bar position surrounded by girls and air-conditioners wasn't as easy as it sounds. I got knock-back after knock-back. Just before sunset, when the old enthusiasm was starting to wane and travelling up and down the streets of Melbourne in the foot Falcon was taking its toll, I cracked it.

It was an extremely posh restaurant in the posh part of town. They were desperate and the manager, who had a personality about as warm as a cane toad, said he'd give me a start as a drinks waiter. It wasn't exactly what I had in mind, but it was a start, a foot in the door. No doubt I could work my way into the bar and rattle up a few cocktails at a later date, once my popularity grew.

'So we'll see you tomorrow at six sharp', he said, 'and I'll expect immaculate attire.'

I said, 'Only the best, mate', took a scan of the place, and headed off back to my budget accommodation in Little Collins.

It was a victory, for sure, but later that night when reality set in I realised I didn't know the first thing about being a waiter. And my arithmetic was shocking, so how was I going to work the change out? The nerves started to grab me a bit and I lay there staring at the ceiling. Someone in the share-kitchen was giving it heaps with the garlic and the fumes were overpowering me, oozing through the gap under the door. It was all getting a bit much. Time for a beer, I decided. I was too uptight to sleep and it would give the garlic fumes time to lift.

Deep in thought, I prowled the pavements, trying to picture myself performing magnificent manoeuvres as a dashing drinks waiter, impressing the up-market clientele with my style. 'He's a bit rough around the edges, but he's got style,' they'd all reckon. I could see it now.

I ducked into a karaoke bar for a charge-up, and I'll be buggered, there was a little Vietnamese bloke singing 'Viva Las Vegas' and he sounded exactly like Elvis. Not bad, I'm thinking, then he goes into 'Green Green Grass of Home' and he sounds exactly like Tom Jones. And then if that wasn't enough, a Whitney Houston song comes on and to the crowd's delight he cranks it out just as if Whitney was singing it, high notes and all. The little bloke was good and so we all powered on until the early hours.

I woke about lunchtime in my budget accommodation with a five-star hangover, shot to pieces. The afternoon slid on and with a few strong coffees and a few yodels I somehow survived. It was getting on and the tension started to mount. I could do it. I'd come through with flying colours. Get confident, I kept telling myself, but the nerves were grabbing me, churning my stomach — I was getting no support from my body at all.

It came time to suit up. First the black pants, way too tight, then the white Glo-weave body shirt which unfortunately emphasised my beer-gut. Then the bow tie, which was so tight I found it hard to draw breath. When I bent over to put on my black Bata Scouts I nearly blacked out. So I walked stiff-legged onto the street, pretty sure my strides were going to rip up the backside at any minute and with the bow tie clamped tight to my windpipe. I was feeling tense.

I covered the 2 kilometres to the restaurant like a bloke who'd accidentally shat himself and was trying to put on a brave front till he found a toilet. I got to the door and was greeted by the manager, Mr Personality. He gave me the once-over and my blood pressure went up, but it couldn't get as far as my head because of the bow tie wrapped around my jugular.

'Table 21 has requested a bottle of Cab Sav and don't forget this restaurant prides itself on professional service and manners of the highest calibre, we are a renowned establishment,' he announced.

I collected my tools — a corkscrew — and headed off, petrified. Stiff-leggedly I made my way past a few tables, toffee-nosed punters looking up, no doubt wondering if I'd swallowed a ping-pong ball and I was walking that way to try to stop it shooting out my arse. I collected the bottle from the barman and headed over to Table 21 which consisted of about ten incredibly posh-looking people. I presented the bottle to the bloke at the head of the table, he gave me the nod and I went for the cork. Steady now, steady . . . but it was too much — the hangover, the bow tie, the nerves, the pressure. With a clumsy, shaky hand I jabbed the corkscrew into the cork with such force it drove the cork straight down the neck of the bottle into the wine. 'Faaaarrrking cork!' I yelled.

I'd never seen ten people swivel their heads around so quickly and in complete unison. It was like a well-trained platoon on the parade ground after they'd just received the command 'Eyes Right'.

Next minute, I was led out the front door by the manager, who politely asked me never to come anywhere near this place ever again.

The door slammed and the emotion of the whole thing hit me hard. I was shattered. I'd failed before in life, but this one cut deep. I tore the bow tie from its stranglehold and drop-kicked it 45 metres onto a tram track, where it was crushed to death by a St Kilda-bound tram. The driver looked as though he couldn't believe I'd kicked it so far. Cop that, you choking bastard, I remember mumbling to myself as I strode off up the street, my pants promptly tearing across my backside. It was one of my most disappointing moments, and that's really saying something when you've got a track record like mine.

Next day at the Greyhound bus terminal the Yugoslav bloke at the counter asked, 'Where would you like to go to, my friend?' With a weakened heart and my head hung low I said, 'You got anything heading north, mate, maybe three or four thousand miles worth?'

Can't Take a Trick

When I really think about it, my form with women over the years has been quite dismal. It's like a racing syndicate that buys a horse and pins all their hopes on it. It comes from a good bloodline, looks good in the paddock, has all the right moves, but never seems to win a race. Frustrating? Yes! Confusing? Yes it sure is! Depressing? Bloody oath, it can be!

Of course there's nights when you're out on the town and you meet some woman and you end up letting the ferret out for a run. And that's great, but it's usually because she's as desperate as you are. When it comes to the ones that really count — you know, that 'special girl' — you can always depend on old No-style O'Brien to completely blow it. I never seem to get past GO. A relationship to me is something that happened to two people in a movie I saw once.

But a little while back I probably could have done all right for myself, if only I'd played my cards right.

A little warning here: if you're prone to depression, maybe you'd better not read the rest of this story. When this certain girl smiled she lit the whole place up, it was like she was hooked up to mains power. Her skin was coffee brown and she had the most beautiful eyes, deep and dark with huge eyelashes. They reminded me of a new-born calf. She was a Maori girl, slim and petite, gentle and soft. She was a transmitter for love and I was receiving loud and clear!

She went by the absolutely glorious name of Leslie Puha.

Fate had brought us together in beautiful forest country. The place and time is irrelevant, the only thing that matters in this story is unadulterated love and the pursuit of happiness. Day in, day out we were working together amidst the pines, Van Morrison cassettes filling the air with passionate expectations, Leslie's occasional glances giving me palpitations. I used to float around all day. I can't honestly remember my feet actually touching the ground at any stage. I would have climbed the highest mountain just for one small sip of Leslie's bath water.

Old Leslie thought I was OK too, I reckon. When we talked she'd gaze into my eyes and the sweet melody of her voice would almost hypnotise me. She was an angel.

One day she emerged out of a crisp early morning forest fog, pressed the play button releasing Van Morrison and asked me if I would like to come over to her farmhouse for dinner that night. I accepted and she seemed to drift off back into the fog again. It was like a dream, a beautiful dream.

The stage was set. Tonight dinner; next week we'd start a family and live happily ever after.

That day finally came to an end and off I took, hitting the showers and polishing up a bit. I made sure not to eat anything, as I knew Leslie would probably cook something really special. So me and the old Holden headed out to Leslie's farmhouse running on love. I was pretty excited, so I tipped a few beers down while I was making the miles to Leslie's farmhouse, probably a few too many.

Leslie was a gracious host, topping my glass up with red and sending me into a spin with every smile that emanated from her beautiful face.

Then came the meal. It was a pasta number. Leslie gave herself a little girly serving and then dumped about five kilos of it in front of me. So I ate the lot just to be polite. I mean, she could have served up a cow pat with a candle on it, I still would have scoffed it just because it came from her kitchen.

To this day I reckon the meat was a bit raw. So there I was — I'd had a heap of beer, red wine and a bucketful of raw mince and pasta and I was really starting to feel it. We had a few more reds, then Leslie came out with a huge mug of milky coffee. I couldn't say no, Leslie was too precious. My stomach started to churn but I thought I had it covered. I was confident I could see this one out. Somehow I got the coffee down but I could feel the perspiration starting to bead on my forehead.

Leslie was so sweet and caring and as it was getting late she suggested I crash on the couch. Well, it had been a nice night we both agreed. So Leslie gave me a blanket and bade me goodnight casually radiating a smile, then casually radiated away into her bedroom.

I lay down for ten minutes, feeling a little crook, a little pissed and a little disappointed. I thought I could have done a bit better. Maybe tried a bit of romance.

Then that voice started in my head, you know the one, the one that keeps telling you — have a crack, have a crack, be cool, she's waiting — forget the couch, forget the couch, be brave, be brave, have a crack!

I resisted for a while but I'm only mortal. I was madly in love and I was convinced Leslie was waiting for me.

That was mistake number one.

Walking into Leslie's room, I soon discovered a side to her personality I didn't know existed. She went off her rocker, to put it mildly, and after a truckload of abuse she spun me around and directed me straight out the door. Pronto. Bang went the door. It wasn't a goer! I don't think I even got a word in.

At this stage I couldn't help but get the impression that the romance was going out of the evening. Slight miscalculation all right, could have happened to anyone. Next thing my stomach started to pump and this time there was no stopping it. The five kilos of raw mince and pasta wanted out and it was going to take the milky coffee and all the beer and the red with it. They were all on the way up and there was no looking back.

I must admit I panicked — it was dark and I didn't know the layout of the house. In a few seconds of sheer terror I couldn't find the toilet, couldn't find the back door. I was in more trouble than the early settlers. It would have to be the kitchen sink! I just made it in time to assume the position and then my whole world exploded, kilos and kilos of it. I spewed like I'd never spewed before. It was commendable how I kept it confined to the sink . . . well, I thought I did anyway.

Next thing was the clean-up. Leslie hadn't fronted, which meant she hadn't heard me. That was a stroke of luck. Now if only I could get rid of the evidence I'd be right.

There was a toothbrush next to the tap so I grabbed it and started poking all the chunky bits down the sink. After a bit of this and a bit of that it looked pretty good. So back to the couch, the place where it all began, the place I should never have bloody left.

With the morning light came complete and inconceivable horror. Leslie was up and she was wild — the last time I saw a haka performed with so much conviction was in the Rugby World Cup. I don't really blame her because the curtains at the window above the sink looked as if they'd been spray-painted with vitamised pizza!

Our relationship never quite recovered from this. Actually, I can't remember Leslie ever talking to me again. Not long after that I left the forest and drifted on. I'd totally blown it with the angel of love.

Somewhere down the track I heard on the grapevine she ended up with a Japanese golf-course manager. Lady Luck must have dealt him some good cards all right, and he obviously played them a bit better than yours truly because I couldn't even take a bloody trick.

The Cavalier Sailor

About this stage in my book I wanted to include an uplifting story, something positive and inspirational. But I couldn't find one. Well, I couldn't find one that involved me anyway. I just don't seem to feature in that kind of story. So instead I thought I'd tell you about a good mate of mine, Mark Johnson (he also pops up later in 'Powelly's Last Ride'), and his journey from rags to riches.

Or in Mark's case, rags to a decent pair of shorts. And fair dinkum, this yarn will point out to all you fellow battlers and eternal optimists that if you stick with it anything's liable to happen, and that there are no boundaries to what a bloke can achieve.

With Mark it all started on the streets of Melbourne, and from what I can gather he was mixing with a pretty rough crowd. An average night on the town for Mark revolved around resuscitating his girlfriend after she'd overdosed. He was in a real rut. He scratched around for years down and out and getting involved with stuff that wasn't worth getting involved with, but he knew deep down he had more to offer and could do better.

The streets of Melbourne had become a jungle and it

was closing in. Then one night Mark dreamed a fantastic dream, a vision of freedom. He was at the helm of a mighty sailing boat, its sails full, its bow slicing through a temperate sea, heading out to nowhere in particular but somewhere spectacular. The dream engulfed his senses completely, intoxicating his subconscious and filling his soul with desire.

Next day, Mark Johnson caught the Greyhound bus.

It wasn't going to be easy. He wasn't cashed up and the streets of Melbourne were all he knew, but he needed to find freedom and he wasn't going to find it there. His ticket got him to the central coast of Queensland, where he kicked around for awhile, did a bit of labouring, then moved on. He stuck to his guns, never looking back. He went north, then he went west, then he went north-east, then south-west, then north again, searching, travelling.

The country opened up for Mark and he felt better than he ever had. He felt the stirrings of freedom starting to well up within, and it felt good. But it wasn't the dream. Could the dream ever become reality he'd often wonder, staring out across the flat. Anyway, he'd keep going, keep looking.

Now when a bloke shows a bit of determination and a bit of guts, there's always the chance, no guarantees, for things to fall into place.

Mark went in many directions, turned his hand to whatever work he could find. He chalked up mile after mile and he remembered the way he felt the morning after the most vivid, colourful dream he'd ever had. Then, as if the script had already been written, the Director of Destiny turned to Mark Johnson and called

'Action'. But there were no cameras and no clapper-board, just the sea breeze and miles of untouched coastline, black smiling faces and warmth, and Mark knew he'd found home. He was born again.

He spent the next few years in that little Territory coastal town and that's where I met him. He really embraced that place and I think he felt life was just beginning for him. He had a flair for carpentry, but he'd never given himself a fair crack at it before, but because he got on so well in the town his confidence grew. No job became too big. Mark became an artist with timber, he'd carve it, chainsaw it, nail it, chisel it and construct it. Soon he was in demand. He'd come a long way from the streets of Melbourne and life couldn't be better. At that time I was still working with the local Aboriginal community on their croc-farming project and living in the caravan on the beach. Mark lived in a shack not far away and we got to spend a fair bit of time together.

The local Aboriginal people also really took Mark in. Hunters and gathers by tradition, they had respect for Mark who in his own way was a hunter and gatherer as well, with skills he'd developed from years of street culture. They shared their knowledge freely and he absorbed it all with a keen interest. I suppose, looking back, it was a good time for all of us — fishing, hunting and plenty of good campfires and cold cans.

Mark never really let too much out of the bag. He seemed happy enough, but reading between the lines I could see he was still restless, still slightly distant. He was still evolving, the journey hadn't been completed, the jigsaw was still unfinished. But only Mark knew which piece to put where. To all of us he was just good old Mark, and no one looked any further or any deeper than the next carton of beer.

So the weeks turned into months and the months turned into the wet season and the wet finally ran out of rain and turned into the warm, windy dry. Stingrays got fat and the turkey bush blossomed and tuna and mackerel moved into the bay.

The dry was a great time for getting out and doing a bit, and the rhythm of life rolled on. I'd just finished another day at the croc farm and, happy to be alive, I positioned myself on a large rock at high tide and cast out a bit of old bait, trying to catch a feed. I hadn't seen Mark for a few days, but that wasn't uncommon, he came and went, just like the wind.

Something caught my eye around the point. I didn't take too much notice because I thought I'd got a nibble on the line. Then I saw this yacht coming round the point. It got closer, and I'll be buggered, it was Mark Johnson. I couldn't believe it. He sailed past, saluted and tacked off into the blue. I couldn't make it out for sure but I think he was dressed in cream-coloured jockettes and a blue cravat.

He tacked, jibbed and went windward, then he jibbed, circumnavigated and shot up and down the deck. A small crowd formed, the binoculars came out and we followed his movements. No one could believe it . . . Mark Johnson had bought a yacht!

He didn't know much about the finer points of sailing, but he somehow kept it off the rocks. And as the sun set, you could see his silhouette racing up and down the deck, adjusting ropes and sails and stuff.

With the wind in his hair, Mark had caught a glimpse of the dream. He was right out there amongst it.

For all us locals, this became the era of the sunset sail. After work we'd all meet and dinghy out to Mark's yacht and proceed to drink salubriously and enjoy the sunset, while Mark took us around the bay teaching himself how to sail. A few cans and everyone became an expert, but Mark stayed focused, he knew what he wanted to achieve.

After a few months he knew his way around that yacht pretty well. It was quite an old yacht, but as he pointed out to me several times, not old like an old Holden, old like a sixties E-type Jag. Its name was *Cavalier Sailor* and it was an impressive sight. Mark and that yacht became one, they lived together, they took on the sea together and they became part of the same dream.

A bit later that year, when he felt in his heart that the time was right, Mark stocked up with rice and two-minute noodles, dug up his passport and decided it was time for the cavalier sailor to meet his fate. He did a sail-past, saluted and headed north. We all farewelled him from the beach, black and white hands waving frantically.

Would he make it? Buggered if I know, was the general response. But we all hoped, and everyone respected Mark's courage for giving it a go.

He sailed for three days and three nights, too scared to sleep. Then on the horizon land loomed, and deliriously Mark poked on towards the greens and browns of the Indonesian island group. It had to be Indonesia he figured, referring to an old school atlas in the cockpit which was his only navigational aid. He anchored in a picturesque little bay. Paradise, he thought to himself, then collapsed, exhausted.

While he slept his mind wandered and he found himself drifting. He dreamt he was lying in a park in Melbourne covered with newspaper and a crowd of people were gawking down at him. The feeling of people watching him annoyed him and he woke prematurely. When he opened his eyes he saw dark faces with half smiles looking back at him from outside the cabin. Indonesian fishermen, curious and friendly. He crawled out of the cabin in his jocks and greeted them.

Mark sailed the islands of Indonesia, slicing through the temperate sea, breathing the freedom and filling his sails, at one with the *Cavalier Sailor*.

Now you're probably wondering, is he just making all this up? I admit it is an amazing story, but life does contain some amazing stories and this one happens to be true. But the journey Mark had undertaken so far was nothing compared to what was about to happen. Although he had no idea, the planets were about to line up for Mark and he was just about to hit the jackpot.

Mark on the Cavalier Sailor.

On an island not far away was a voluptuous Bavarian backpacker. Her name was Maria von Love. She was a big-breasted, beer-making woman who emanated love. It shone out of her like a beacon. She was kind and gentle, with the sun in her smile and an itching in her feet. She stood like a Viking queen amongst the Indonesians at the central village market. Mark had come ashore looking to buy some fresh fruit and a little spice to put on his fish. Maria was standing there, next to the paw paw.

It was no use resisting, because it was bigger than both of them. They fell hopelessly in love.

Like players in a fairy tale, they sailed off together. And as the sunset melted away into one hundred soft shades of pastel, they made love for the first time, on the bow of the *Cavalier Sailor*.

Mark hadn't been with a woman for years. He'd never been with a woman like Maria von Love and he found the moment almost overwhelming. He looked into her eyes, sea breeze caressing the moment, and he heard himself gently whisper, 'Maria, life's just begun.' And for both of them . . . it had.

The Movie Mob

Not many people realise this, but I have actually graced the silver screen. Not a big role, but I think it was fairly riveting. I just had to poke my beer-gut out and this other bloke gave it a pat and said, 'You wouldn't want to end up with one of these now, would you?' It was a television ad promoting low-alcohol beer, and my bit featured right at the end. Me and my beer-gut were meant to be the deterring factor — if you drink too much full-strength beer you end up looking like me. A bit humiliating. It was a short, sharp career, although I think one mob was interested in my beer-gut to do a bit of modelling for one of those shops that sell clothes for oversize blokes.

But like a lot of other great actors, I made the transition from being in front of the camera to working behind the scenes. It was when a big movie production came to the Northern Territory — the movie was called *Yolngu Boy*. Aboriginal people from the north-east corner of the Northern Territory call themselves Yolngu and the movie was about three young Yolngus journey through life.

At the time I was just poking around like I normally do, not achieving much but as usual managing to scrape by. Filming had just started on *Yolngu Boy*, there were trucks and gear going all over the place and a whole host of new faces turned up in town. She was a big production.

The acting force was the local Yolngu, except for two young fellas from the Tiwi Islands. For such a relatively small group of people the Yolngu over the years have produced some top footballers, world-class artists and musicians, and craftsmen and bushmen of note. And now they were going to turn their hand to acting. They are a flamboyant people, and I was glad I ended up being dragged into the project as well. The movie-making mob had heard on the grapevine that I'd had over two hundred jobs and amounted to nothing, but they'd also heard that I knew pretty well everyone in the area, so they asked me if I wanted to be the Cast Coordinator.

Now how can a bloke knock back a job with a title like that? I told the head guy this was my destiny, I was born to be a Cast Coordinator. I would coordinate anything that came within a 100-kilometre radius of my position on the planet. Although I didn't realise it at the time, Cast Coordinator is pronounced 'taxi driver'.

The film set was all go when I pulled up there the next morning. People flying around yelling into walkie-talkies, scaffolds going up, huge lights, trucks, cameras, trailers and more people yelling into walkie-talkies. A bloke on a four-wheel motorbike roared past and he was yelling into a walkie-talkie as well. I was promptly issued with a walkie-talkie by the casting director, who introduced me to the first director, who introduced me to the second director and the third director, who introduced me to his mate who reckoned he should have been a director, who introduced me to the producer, who had a son training to be a director.

They were all concerned because they needed a live goanna for one of the hunting scenes later that day and the only one they could find didn't have a tail. A bloke from the props department rushed up with a rubber tail and was getting organised to glue it on, which brought a sigh of relief from the crew. No one wanted a tail-less goanna.

They were a very focused mob of people and the whole thing was run like a military operation. Go, go, go, action, roll 'em — and my job was to find 'em. The whole thing had to run like clockwork to meet the budget and everything was planned down to the last minute. Now this was fine, but Yolngu people don't measure time in seconds, minutes and hours. They'd rather look at time in days and seasons. They operate in Yolngu time. When it happens, it happens. That philosophy has worked for thousands of years and it's a healthy, uncomplicated way of life.

As the Cast Coordinator, I found myself caught in the middle of things a bit. On one hand I had the film mob who just wanted to roll it, wrap it and get it in the can, and on the other hand I had the Yolngu cast who wanted to hunt stingray because the tide was right, and maybe do a bit of acting later, maybe the next day.

I had no time to wallow in the glory of being called Cast Coordinator. I had actors to find. So I was fair dinkum flat out like a dead donkey's donger, driving all around town, door-knocking through the community, following footprints in the sand and even searching the mangroves because one bloke, meant to be acting, decided to go crabbing with the family.

Some of the Yolngu were punctual and fronted up to the set on time. But in this uniquely beautiful part of Australia, life's for living and although everyone was genuinely excited about the movie, there's a lot of other activities that concern Aboriginal people and their day-to-day life in the community. For example, there are the ongoing ceremonial responsibilities that take preference over just about everything else. And there's the family — family bonds and commitments are very important. No matter what else is happening at the time, family business is always a priority. But all up, the Yolngu were doing a great job with the actual acting, and after a while we got a bit of a routine going.

The film mob gave me a schedule so I knew who had to be on the set at certain times. Once I'd picked up the cast for that shoot and got them to the set, they had to go straight to Star wagon. Now, Star wagon was a bus on the outside, but on the inside it was a fully modernised beauty parlour and hairdressing salon at one end and a clothes boutique at the other. Star wagon was the first port of call for the actors. They'd get decked out in the appropriate outfit and get a bit of a polish-up from the make-up lady, then go onto the set for a bit of Academy Award stuff.

Star wagon also towed a toilet around but most people, including me, were too scared to use it, because you'd go in and you'd be sitting in there and next minute the whole film set, including Star wagon, would decide to move off at great speed to the next location. When you came out you found yourself ten miles away from where you went in.

After a few weeks of it all, I was pretty well exhausted both mentally and physically. I was burning out. All the film mob had motel rooms except me. By the time I was hired there were none left so I had to just camp out on the edge of town like an old derro. It didn't really worry me, but the sandflies were particularly bad there, so I wasn't getting much sleep. But the cogs kept turning and the movie mob ticked over like a well-oiled machine. They were rolling and wrapping, cameramen were firing from the hip, and the caterers were turning out great tucker. The Yolngu actors were performing well and were a credit.

But the black cat that's been following me around for most of my life decided to run out in front of my Toyota. And once again I failed to run it over, and bad luck was thus bestowed upon me.

After a really hectic day tracking one of the cast members for hours who'd taken off fishing, and then copping a blast from the wardrobe lady because all the actors were going home in their outfits from Star wagon instead of bringing them back, I decided I'd earned myself a decent coffee. So I pulled into the movie mob's makeshift office and headed straight for the coffee plunger. Now the coffee plunger held about seven to eight cups, so I filled it up with boiling water and a big heap of coffee and was getting set to down the lot. I pushed the plunger down and BANG! The glass broke and boiling coffee erupted out all over my leg. It hit slightly south of my left plum and burnt all the way down my leg to my foot.

I was in shock for a moment, coffee sizzling away against my skin. Then I let out a hoot that sounded like the mating call of a spinifex pigeon played backwards. Next minute a young cameraman runs out to see what's happened and we took off to the hospital. I tried to put on a brave face but the pain was pretty severe, especially around the tender groin area. With every minute the pain got more intense and I can only thank me lucky stars my scrotum missed out.

They got me into Emergency and the doctor checked it out and they packed it in ice and gave me some pain-killers. By now my leg was starting to look a bit like a piece of pork crackling. There goes my modelling career, I'm thinking. It's funny, you know, of all the things that could have put me in hospital over the years, all the near misses, all the lucky escapes, it's the coffee plunger that finally puts a bloke away. As they were wheeling me down the corridor to my hospital room I tried to look on the bright side of things. OK, I said to myself, the pain's excruciating, you're in a hospital for the first time, it's all feeling very strange, but hang on . . . what about the nurses?

You don't have to be Dr Zhivago to work out there's bound to be some really nice nurses around, and me being a patient in pain I'm bound to get a bit of a pampering. You could put money on that, I'm thinking as the orderly parked me in some room. The nurses will be along any minute, they'll probably want to sponge me down after my ordeal, then they'll probably want to massage my nerve endings and reassure me and gently put the cup to my lips for a sip of water. With that sort of treatment, I'll pull through.

Well, I waited, and I stayed up all night, lying there waiting, my leg packed in ice like a six-pack. The only nurse that turned up was a male nurse around four in the morning. He told me he was knocking off and his mate, another male nurse, would be in soon to see if I needed anything.

All of a sudden I went off the idea of a sponge-down. What's a burn victim got to do to get pampered by a female nurse around here? Every other hospital in the southern hemisphere had them.

As the sun gingerly poked its first rays over the horizon and another day was about to break, things were already stirring on the *Yolngu Boy* film set. The caterers were hard at it, and the trucks were rolling in, and the walkie-talkies were coming out.

But there'd be no Cast Coordinator fronting up that morning. The old Cast Coordinator was getting burn cream rubbed around his groin area by a male nurse whose hands seemed to be going just that little bit too close to his plums. And I'm thinking, not only is this an adventure that got me absolutely nowhere, it's also a really lousy way for a Cast Coordinator to start the day.

Ben Hur — a Croc in Love

Collecting crocodile eggs is one thing, but collecting the crocodiles themselves is another matter. Trying to catch crocs at night isn't something you do for a bit of fun. It's not like having a few coldies on the beach, or watching the cricket. It's a fairly serious way to spend an evening. But there I was, doing my duty as a croc farmer, trying to build up a bit of breeding stock. I can honestly say there's two things you constantly think of when you're poking around in a little dinghy up some black, tepid, shitty swamp looking for a croc. First, you wish you had a bigger boat, and secondly, you wish you were a long way away doing something else.

The technique we used was the spotlight and harpoon method. One bloke scans the waterway with an extremely bright spotlight, slowly panning from left to right till the telltale red glow of a crocodile's eyes are caught in the light. It's incredible how a croc's eyes will glow when picked up by the spotty — they can be hundreds of metres off but the red-eye shine is unmistakable. Once you've located a croc you slowly approach, keeping the spotlight directly on it. This must mesmerise the croc a bit because they generally don't move much. Sometimes they'll go under the water but mostly they're pretty transfixed by the light.

The next step takes a lot of care and concentration and you have to put the beer you wish you were having completely out of your mind.

A harpoon is prepared, ready to drive into the croc. Usually you aim for the loose roll of skin at the back of the neck. The harpoon is a long pole with two small barbed steel prongs at the end. The prongs are also attached to a coil of light cord or rope. Slowly you motor up to the croc with the boat, spotty right on it, and when you're pretty well next to it you drive the harpoon in.

This doesn't actually damage the croc. The prong goes in only a short way, and the pole comes off and you throw that back in the boat, and then pick up the coil of rope and play the croc like a fish. The croc's first move usually is to go under the water and head for the bottom and just sit there. If it's not a real big croc you can try to pull it in. But if it's got any size on it you can run the risk of pulling the barbs out and then you've lost him. So you have to go steady and wait till it comes up for a breath, then start trying to get it up to the boat. Depending how stressed it is the croc might stay down half an hour or so before it surfaces.

A cat-and-mouse game can go on for hours if it's a big one, and a croc only gets big if it's a bit smarter than the other ones.

One particular night I had a feeling we were dealing with something a little special. We finally pulled him up against the side of the boat and he was strong and mean.

He went into a roll, which was good for us. Rolling the body is a ploy that crocs use for attack and also defence. A death roll can be used to break its prey's bones and drown it, and if a croc is in a fight or in a pressured situation it will also roll its body. This worked for us because the croc wrapped himself up a bit in the harpoon rope and we managed to get another rope around his snout as well and tie it shut. One good trick at this stage is to put a blindfold around their eyes. This seems to settle them down a bit.

Crocs, when they're under pressure, make a terrible guttural groaning sound. On this memorable night our croc groaned the ghastliest groan I'd ever heard. It echoed up my spine, around the mangroves, down the creek, back up my spine and across the bay. Translated, that groan meant something along the lines of, 'If this rope holding my jaws shut slips off, I'll tear off at least one of your limbs and possibly your head as well.'

So amidst a chorus of 'Do we really have to be here?' and 'If I survive this I'm going to drink for a week', you perform the big heave-ho and drag the croc into the boat. It thrashes and twists, and at this stage I don't know who's more stressed out, me or the croc. We called this croc Ben Hur because like the movie production of the same name he was big, but not only that, he had a bad attitude. I'd say with my modest experience of crocs, that Ben, if he hadn't already eaten anyone, was definitely the type of croc that would take someone. I know it took a few years off my life trying to tie up the big scaly bastard.

My good mate and local wildlife officer Mark Stevens was an expert at this operation and he showed me a fair bit. He was a very reliable bloke to work with, and we

Mark Stevens and Phil tying up a small croc.

had a lot in common — he liked his beer just as much as I did. So after the joy of getting Ben tied up and into the tinny, and the laugh-a-minute fun time getting him from the tinny to the croc farm ute, there was only one more carefully calculated part of the operation left, and that was the drive-in bottle shop. Time to give the old nervous system a bit of a stabiliser.

Unfortunately, Ben Hur was too big for the ute and his tail was hanging out the back, which scared the shit out of the bottle-shop attendant. Ben was already making a name for himself around town . . .

Back at the farm, as with any croc we caught, I measured him and sexed him just for the records. Sexing a croc is quite an interesting procedure. You have to stick your finger fair up the croc's clacker valve. After inserting the finger you feel around a bit for a penis. If you can't feel one it's generally a female. Now this always gets a serious reaction out of the croc, and a slightly higher-pitched groan as well. Of course you only do this while it's securely tied up.

Big Ben Hur was all male, there was no doubt about it. We released him into a natural billabong area at the back of the farm. There were several other crocs in there as well and it had a good solid fence going around it. Right from the start Ben Hur didn't take to captivity and to show his resentment he went on a rampage, killing half the living things in there. He was completely out of control. After about a week the once-quiet, picturesque natural billabong area of the farm resembled the killing floor at Katherine Meatworks. There were bones and guts lying around everywhere. There was no stopping the beast.

We went out spotlighting again and caught another croc in the bay, as we needed to get the numbers back up. But Ben's killfest continued and next day the new croc was just a headless corpse floating belly up in the once tranquil billabong. Somehow we had to stop this

An unsuspecting croc just before his head was bitten off.

slaughter, but I was buggered if I knew how. As quick as we were catching them, Ben was dismantling them. Of course there was the suggestion of shooting him right between the eyes, but as tempting as that sounded it wouldn't work because Ben was just too bloody cunning. You only had to go anywhere near the billabong and he'd duck under the water and you wouldn't know where he was. He pretty well had us euchred.

Without a doubt, crocs each have their own personality, just like dogs or horses. Some are more aggressive than others, some seem almost dopey. But old Ben was the most rogue thing I'd ever come across. I've no doubt he would have chewed on his own mother just for something to do. He was a serial killer, and he was having the time of his life.

When all hope seemed lost the most amazing thing happened. Ben Hur decided to pull a stunt that could only be described as bloody spectacular. Whether he had it planned or it was just off the cuff, no one will ever know.

During the night he crawled out of the billabong and made his way across to the fence and ate a hole in it big enough to drive a car through. He then marched into another pen that held three crocs, a big male called Wally Gator and two females, Laverne and Shirley. Ben flogged the hell out of Wally then he hunted the two females back through the hole he'd eaten in the fence and back to the billabong. Obviously Ben was in the mood for love.

The next morning me and the boys turned up for work and thought we'd check on the latest carnage down at the billabong. We were stunned. One of the females Ben had busted out the night before, Laverne, was

The lovely Laverne and Shirley.

sunning herself on the bank and there was Ben just bobbing around in front of her, butter wouldn't melt in his jaws, swimming up and down like a love-sick pup. He'd do some funny manoeuvre then look around at her, then some other funny manoeuvre then look back, just to make sure she was watching. He was gone, he was love-struck. He wasn't interested in the other female, Shirley, just Laverne. She was the one for him.

We examined the hole in the fence and saw Wally Gator lying there, bark off him everywhere, in a bad way. The tracks in the sand told the whole story: how Ben had come up from the billabong, the eating of the fence, the fight, then taking Laverne and Shirley back to the billabong. Pretty romantic stuff for a crocodile. It reminded me of an Elvis movie — you know, Elvis meets girl, beats up existing boyfriend, wins over girl . . .

Ben never hurt another croc while I was at the farm. He underwent a complete personality change. He put it all behind him, he settled down. Not only did he dote on Laverne constantly, but when it was feeding time — the big test for any croc — he'd let her eat first then he'd nibble away at the scraps. He'd actually gone pretty soppy. That just goes to show you the power of love, doesn't it?

This was a love affair jam-packed with emotion, chivalry, adventure and total commitment. Probably one of the greatest love stories of modern days, and I felt honoured to have played a small part. No one would ever suspect a croc could be capable of love, no way, not in this day of scientific rationality. You ask any expert: crocs don't have emotions, they don't care, they're just instinctive killing machines.

But Ben was the exception I reckon, and I don't care what any expert says, that lizard really did his nuts!

Fifteen Minutes of Fame

These days I don't really have a permanent place of abode. Wherever the old Toyota pulls up is home, so it's pretty well 'No fixed address'. Whenever I have to fill out a form that requires 'Address', I generally put down the rego number of my old Toyota, and that's about the best I can do.

But it hasn't always been like that. I've had periods where I've settled down here and there and lived a normal kind of life for a while. Working on the Yolngu community's croc farm for two or three years was a 'settled' period — before itchy-feet syndrome caught up with me. While there, I lived in a caravan on a beach at a place called Drimmie Head. This was a period in my life when a lot of crazy things happened, but apart from that some good friendships were forged as well.

My neighbour on the next beach was Mandawuy Yunupingu. Munda, as he's known locally, lived there with his family and has made a name for himself as front man for the rock band Yothu Yindi. The year I was Munda's neighbour was 1992, the year he was chosen as

Australian of the Year, and he was doing a lot of work around Australia and the world with Yothu Yindi and also as a statesman for Aboriginal people. No matter how hectic Munda's schedule was he always had time for a beer and a yarn, and if there was a guitar around Munda would play request after request unselfishly for whoever wanted to listen. He was totally unaffected by fame and his increasingly high public profile.

Munda was a good bloke, and many a night was spent around a campfire sharing songs and philosophies and thoughts for the future. Munda knew I was a passionate musician and he also knew I could play only three chords and wasn't really much chop. But he'd give me all the encouragement in the world and try to get me going a bit.

One day Munda rocks up to the croc farm where I'm working and says his mate Jimmy Barnes is coming up with his family and could I pick them up at the airport? I couldn't believe it. Jimmy Barnes, the great rock-and-roller — this was going to be the highlight of my musical career! I think Munda knew I'd get a real kick out of meeting Jimmy and he probably figured it might inspire me to go and learn that fourth chord. So he said to take the brand-new Toyota Landcruiser that the community had just purchased, the pride of the fleet.

Now, being a brand-new vehicle no one worried about checking the oil, and when I went to pick it up I didn't worry about checking the oil either, because it was a brand-new vehicle. I headed out to the little airport late in the arvo, all set to pick up superstar Jimmy Barnes and family. The new Toyota just purred and it was a real slice of heaven covering the thirty-odd kilometres with the air-con on full blast.

When I got to the airport it all started to sink in and my stomach started to knot up with nerves and excitement. It's not every day I get a job like this and by the time the jet landed I was so worked up I thought I'd be battling to string a sentence together. Anyway, it all happened quickly, one minute I'm nerve-struck, then all of a sudden there's Jimmy Barnes and family and we're chewing the fat. You couldn't help but relax, because he was such a good sort of bloke, friendly, easy-going, and his wife was lovely and the kids were really well-mannered, pleasant kids. All up they were just a bloody nice family unit. So I settled down a bit.

Apparently the kids had their own band going called the Tin Lids and they'd come up to do a film clip with Munda's kids. The song was called 'The School Song' and they were going to release it fairly soon. The whole family were pretty happy to be out of the Big Smoke for a while and were looking forward to a good week. As we cruised along heading back to Drimmie Head, I was just about to tell Jimmy I knew three chords and was also a dedicated musician — stuff he really needed to know, the same stuff every clown who meets him probably goes on about. But he was spared that because the Toyota blew up. Smoke billowed out from under the bonnet and the brand-new Toyota came to a grinding, smoking, rattling, sizzling halt. The motor had seized and it was all over.

By the time I'd got out and lifted the bonnet Jimmy and his family had disappeared. They were out of the vehicle in a second and into the hire car that was following us, driven by the Yothu Yindi manager who'd been out at the airport as well, making sure everything went smoothly. I felt pretty embarrassed as they drove off leaving me standing there with the smoking hulk. Bad luck had defeated me once again.

Two hours later someone came back, and we towed the Toyota carcass back to Drimmie Head and I managed to catch the last part of the welcome party for Jimmy and family. I don't know what impression I made on Jimmy and his lovely family. At a rough guess I'd say they probably thought I was a drop-kick, but a few days later I got the chance to really redeem myself.

They all rocked up with the film crew to the croc farm where I was toiling away, and wanted to know if I could feed a fish to the biggest croc while they filmed it. They thought it might look good in their film clip for 'The School Song'. This was my big chance to contribute something to their project. I could see it now: first a fish, then Jimmy would probably ask me to join his band. You didn't have to be Andy Warhol to work out my fifteen minutes of fame had finally come around.

I took a good-sized trevally from the chiller and had a meeting with the camera crew. I told them to trust me because I knew these crocs, and being with them day in, day out, I understood their behavioural patterns and how they'd react in certain situations. I raved on and even impressed myself — did I really know all that?

I tuned the cameraman right in and the film crew thought I knew what I was talking about. The plan was that I would stand at one end of the pen and feed our biggest croc the trevally. Obviously the camera guy wanted to get a good view of the action, so I confidently told him to climb in down the other end of the pen. 'All the croc's going to be thinking about is the trevally,' I pointed out. 'So he's not even going to notice you down the other end filming. No problems.' The camera guy was a bit toey, but I reassured him, 'Just trust me.'

Once I figured everyone knew what was going on, I opened the mesh gate and got the attention of the huge croc inside. As that was the only gate, the cameraman had to actually climb over the fence with his gear down the other end and get ready for the shot.

Everything was going well, the croc was moving down towards me and I was all set to feed him the trevally. Then the cameraman jumped off the fence and landed in the pen ready to film. The croc picked up the vibrations of him jumping in and spun around and started heading straight for him, probably with the intention of tearing him limb from limb. The camera bloke froze with a look on his face that said, 'Hey, this isn't in the script!'

The croc's picking up pace so I yelled, 'Jump out! Quick! Get out!' The camera bloke tried to climb out but he panicked and couldn't get his footing on the mesh fence, and he's in all sorts of strife with the croc bearing down on him. 'Quick, quick, quick!' we were all yelling, but it was too late, he wasn't going to get it together. So I took my life in my hands and ran after the croc and belted him in the head with the trevally, and he turned and came after me. I took off back to the safety of the gate with the croc on me hammer, and somewhere along the line the croc got the trevally, I got to the gate, the cameraman climbed out, and no one had filmed anything.

It really was touch-and-go. I felt bad because I'd miscalculated. But it could have happened to anyone, I'm thinking. Not being a courageous person by nature I was a bit rattled, so we went to Plan B. This time I was to open the gate and feed a fish to the now quite excited croc, with the cameraman behind me. This all went a lot better. The croc came up, got the fish and the bloke filmed it all from behind me, not actually anywhere near the croc or any danger.

The only bloke who was in any danger was me feeding the croc the fish but it was worth it, I'm thinking. It's well worth a little danger if you're going to be an important part of someone's video clip. If you're going to be centre-stage, what's a little risk? If everyone's entitled to fifteen minutes of fame, you might as well get what's owing to you. You might as well use it up.

So two months later when I saw the video clip come on TV, I'm thinking, this is it, my big part should be coming on any moment. It was really exciting. So there's me squinting away at the screen . . . flash! . . . hey, was that my back? And that was it. Me from behind for a split second. I thought I saw a fish in my hand, but my bit was over so quickly I couldn't really tell.

All that danger for a split second and you didn't even see the croc. That's showbiz, I suppose. Obviously most of my stuff ended up on the editing-room floor. Probably too many rude gestures between me and the cameraman.

But there was no point getting despondent, or even thinking it was an adventure that got me nowhere, because it was great actually meeting Jimmy Barnes and his family. And it was a nice gesture from Munda to involve me in all this. And to look on the bright side: OK, I only had one split second of fame but according to my calculations, I've still got fourteen minutes and fifty-nine seconds up my sleeve. That's going to come in really handy one day!

Private Enterprise

No point saying I was doing it tough at the time because, mate, that would've been an understatement. I was going through my darkest financial hour, a total solar eclipse of the wallet.

I was camped in the bush, just out from a small coastal town in the Northern Territory. Down to my last two bits of dried-out bread and a drop of old golden syrup in a tub. Well, it could be worse, I'm thinking, trying to keep my spirits up. Don't exactly know how, but I suppose things could be worse. So I walked away from my camp to take a leak and a crow swept in from nowhere, grabbed my tub of golden syrup and flew off with it. Things were worse.

So after walking around grimacing for a while, I sat down and wrote my thirteenth song, called 'Never Underestimate the Power of Bad Luck', which made me feel even lower.

The next few days I really had to tighten the belt. I mean physically, to stop my pants from falling down, because there were a lot more dinnertimes than dinners. If not for a good Samaritan coming past one day and giving me a fish, I would have done it even leaner. Hawks were starting to circle overhead above my camp. And that's no joke.

But it's times like these that put a bit of fire in your belly. You get that far down, there just isn't anywhere else further down to go. And so you start thinking about going up. So I set out again on the fickle journey of life, one thing led to another, and I chanced to pick up some timely work with a plumber bloke. He had a heap of work on and so the next few months found me either on the shovel or hooking disposable nappies out of septic systems.

Believe it or not, I actually saved a bit of money and I was dead-set determined never to be broke again. No more scrapes. No, thanks. I was on the way up and I had to keep on going up, I thought to myself. I figured it was usually the self-employed people who made the real money, so I started to think along those lines. 'Tourism's on the up in the Territory' all the front-bar scholars were pointing out to me. I was all hyped up ready to go. Phil

Phil O'Brien Safaris hits the road. Me and the old Toyota.

O'Brien Safaris — it had an air of professionalism about it — 'Phil O'Brien Safaris, go anywhere'. Better than going nowhere!

It wasn't so stupid — I mean, I go anywhere anyway, may as well take a few paying tourists along and make money out of it. So I sat down and studied the form a bit. I had a four-wheel drive and some camping gear, and I knew my way around pretty well, so it was all feasible. I could just picture it — I'd never be broke ever again.

Next step, I got some public liability cover and registered a business name, because I decided to do this all above board. Starting my own business had been a bit of a dream for a long time, so I wanted to kick off all legal-like, and keep things that way. I based myself in Katherine, and having always had a soft spot for Kakadu I thought I'd make that my big safari destination. In years gone past I'd worked as a tour guide briefly for a few other companies, and I'd had my ups and downs and got into all sorts of strife. But this was different, this was to be a mature, calculated business venture.

On paper it was a real winner. I would feed them corned beef and damper till it came out their ears, show them the sights, and then get the guitar out and sing them my repertoire of thirteen songs under the moonlight. I was planning to impact on Territory tourism in a huge way. So when the first Phil O'Brien safari was due to leave Katherine, the air was full of optimism, just like when they launched the *Titanic*. What could possibly go wrong?

I was fully registered, insured and accredited and had every permit north of the Tropic of Capricorn. Bad luck — I could find only one paying passenger who wanted to go with me. But that's no problem, because this first trip was basically a reconnaissance trip anyway, I'm thinking. The fact that I was nearly broke after paying all that insurance and stuff didn't really faze me either, because once the word was out that I was a top operator, the big money would roll in soon enough. No worries about that one. So into the early morning light we poked off, me and my one passenger.

She was ravishing. A tall, dark, sophisticated English girl in her early twenties. At first glance she seemed to possess a very gentle, delicate nature, extreeeeemely well spoken and immaculately dressed and with a touch of class. I took her two hundred and ninety-nine dollars and had a good feeling about her straight up. First trip and I get a supermodel. She assured me in her refined English accent that she loved nature and had always wanted to do a genuine Eco-tour.

We reached Mary River Roadhouse at the southern entrance to Kakadu and I said, 'I'll buy a carton and some ice.'

She said politely, 'Actually, I'm more of a scotch-drinker.'

'No problems,' I said, Mr High-Roller, 'I'll get a bottle of that as well.' The English Eco-Rose will probably only have a few eco-sips anyway, I'm thinking, should last the whole four days of the trip.

Now that was probably one of my biggest miscalculations ever. She started cracking cans before we even pulled out of the Mary River Roadhouse carpark. She power-drank her way through the first three, guzzled number four and then sucked five and six, and I'm thinking, wow, this girl's got spunk!

I pulled up at the camping spot just as she was reaching for the next six-pack. I'd picked a beautiful place at the base of the escarpment, complemented by an exquisite little waterfall. 'This calls for a drink,' she said, and wopped another one down. I figured I'd better bang a feed into her pretty quick or else at the rate she was downing the grog, she'd be choked out before the sun went down.

So I set up my new plastic picnic table, then got out my state-of-the-art new gas cooker. Not your old gas-bottle job, this thing had a gas cylinder and cooking element all built in. If there's one thing Phil O'Brien Safaris prides itself on, it's modern camping technology. I put the frypan on and arked the rig up and threw two choice kangaroo fillets on. And started sizzling. All this must have really impressed my English tourist because in between skulls she's yelling, 'Flombay, oh yeah, flombay,' waving her can around, cheering me on.

She was having a great time. I didn't know what flombay meant, but I did notice that the new gas cooking turnout had a really good flame. It was really giving off some heat! Unfortunately, the reason it had such a great flame was because my new plastic picnic table it was sitting on was on fire. Next minute, the table's a fiery molten mass of burning plastic and before I could do anything the gas burner and the roo fillets were engulfed as well. All that was left by the time I'd smothered it out with a blanket were two legs of the table and a molten blob with a smoking gas cylinder sticking out. Which, to its credit, never blew up.

'Man, that's really cooking,' she said.

I apologised but she said, 'Don't worry,' as she tore the top off another coldie. I don't know where she was putting it all. I figured she was just letting her hair down. Anyway it was her tour and Phil O'Brien Safaris was there to provide a professional and unforgettable bush experience.

So far I'd delivered on the unforgettable, that was for sure. As there was still a bit of daylight left I took her for a walk up the escarpment to watch the sunset. You know, let the smoke clear from the big meltdown and maybe talk about the flora and fauna and hopefully bang on a bit of the old eco. It was a typically beautiful sunset and several beers later we were trying to climb down in the dark as I'd forgotten the torch. By now I'd had a few as well so by the time we reached the bottom we hadn't broken any records for the quickest descent.

Back at the camp she went straight for the esky. But that was empty and I was hoping she'd forgotten about the bottle of scotch. No way, she had the top off, threw some ice in a pannikin, wopped the scotch in, and she's into it, just tipping it straight down. She obviously appreciated a good scotch. In between gulps she'd give it a gargle, just savouring it, and the noise would echo out around the base of the escarpment. I could just imagine all the small nocturnal marsupials in the area wondering, 'What the hell was that?'

I lit a fire and had a pannikin with her, just before she drained the bottle. She was a likeable girl, and believe it or not she was still coherent. So I thought I'd better finish off Day One of the tour in a professional manner and put my new tent up.

Eco-girl was just gazing up at the veil of stars, totally at one with the universe, but starting to look a bit eco-ed out. I got stuck into my new tent, but had no idea how to put it up.

Then I heard 'boomp' and I looked around and she's on her back, sprawled out like a human starfish, mouth wide open and starting to snore with an English accent. Well, she'd had a real big day. I got stuck back into the tent — it was a nightmare but I eventually got it up. It took a good hour and I was serenaded the whole time by her steady snoring. She sounded like a 3Kva generator.

I dragged her across the ground and into the tent, rolled her onto her swag and covered her up. No one can say Phil O'Brien Safaris don't care for their clients. I myself crashed under the stars, and slept the deep sleep of a man who was destined never to be broke ever again. A secure, confident, self-employed, financially viable sleep, dreaming the dreams of success.

At first light I sprang up and cleaned the empties away. It looked like there'd been a bucks' party the night before. I kicked a bit of sand over the former new picnic table remains and the camp looked pretty good in the misty early morning.

Miss Eco-guzzler lifted herself up out of the swag, and much to my surprise was pretty chirpy. Not a bad effort after drinking enough alcohol to pickle the inner organs of an emu. She'd absorbed that carton and scotch like a deep-sea sponge, but she was smiling away.

I'm thinking, what great company, as I launched myself into a full Phil O'Brien Safaris continental breakfast — billy tea and toast. She thought it was great. To look at her you'd think butter wouldn't melt in her mouth, but I tell you what, she knew how to hang off a can.

Soon enough the sun started to gently emerge over the peak of the escarpment, illuminating the different shades of green among the woodland, spreading out across the flat and highlighting the colours in the sandstone face of the age-old ranges.

The bush was now totally awake. Lorikeets had clocked on and had started working on the blossoms in the paperbarks, geckos were slogging it out in the leaf litter and the odd crow was giving it the old wark-wark, ever optimistic that something might get run over somewhere nearby.

We worked our way through the day's itinerary, highlighted by a late-afternoon boat cruise on a billabong full of amazing birdlife, luscious scenery and a bit of action from the many crocs that inhabited the area.

It couldn't have been a better day, so on a bit of a high I suggested on our way back to the camp we stop in at a little bush resort and grab a six-pack to have with the spectacular feed I was planning. Her face lit up like a footy park during a night match. 'What a simply delightful idea,' she said.

When we got to the resort it was so expensive to just buy a six-pack that it made more sense to buy a slab. In the long run it worked out a lot cheaper.

'Oh yes,' she agreed, 'it makes a lot more sense to get the whole carton ... and is that Jameson's scotch up there, Phil? That's a really super, smashing scotch.'

What the hell, I thought, I doubt she'd siphon it off like she did the night before, it couldn't be possible, she was only flesh and blood. So I got the lot, money flying out my pockets left, right and centre. I'd forgotten I'd shouted the boat cruise as well.

Back at the camp I knocked up one of my special dishes on the fire, johnnycakes and steak with a generous garnish of my favourite herb, salt. She downed eight cans before tea, ripped the steak apart and without missing a beat went onto number nine. I thought I'd better grab a beer before they were all gone. Drinking good cold beer camped out in the bush really is one of the simple joys in life. She obviously felt the same way.

So there we were under the stars, getting stuck into it, and somewhere between the slab and the scotch I remembered I was actually a professional tour operator and had better get the tent up. I gave Miss Eco-sponge the binoculars and suggested she do a bit of stargazing. I started with the tent and then I heard 'boomp'. I looked around and she'd passed out, but this time she'd stayed on her stool . . . sort of. Her backside was still on the

Phil O'Brien, professional tour operator.

stool, with her legs spread out in front of her. But she'd fallen back and her head was hanging down on the ground with her arms spread out behind her.

In the dark she looked like a giant crab with a pair of binoculars balancing on top of it. Even though I was half-cut I managed to think with some clarity, so I pitched the tent right alongside her, unzipped it, laid her swag out and tipped her in. I'd really started to warm to this girl and I think she felt the same way about me. But it's funny, it wasn't a physical thing, nothing like that was on the agenda. It was more like the common interests we shared . . . a genuine feeling for the bush and a passion for drinking in the bush.

The next couple of days saw the Phil O'Brien Safaris wheels virtually fall off. Flora and fauna became a thing of the past. It was just me and her wandering around having a good time. We were like two innocent butterflies frolicking through the garden of the nicest country in the world, cracking many cans as we went. What was meant to be a four-day trip eased into a fifth day and her two hundred and ninety-nine dollars was long spent. But I suppose the straw that broke the camel's credit rating was when we eventually left Kakadu — I think it was Day Seven by then — and we're cruising along when she saw a sign saying 'Litchfield National Park', which happened to be pointing in the opposite direction.

'Oh Phil, I've heard so much about that place,' she cooed.

Personally I've never been well known for discipline, and we were having such a good time, and it's no point trying to hoard money — I mean, you can't take it with you.

Three more enjoyable Litchfield days later, we're finally pulling into Darwin Airport carpark and she's due to catch a plane back to London. I had to borrow three dollars off her to pay for the parking. She'd had an absolutely wonderful eco-tour, she said with a tear in her eye. 'It was super, Phil,' she called out as she skipped off in the direction of the international passenger lounge. 'See you in London.' And she was gone.

Now to say I was stony broke doesn't come anywhere near describing my financial situation at the time. I'd gone under. Phil O'Brien Safaris never sailed again. There was no second trip. It was over.

My big business venture fizzled, but I tell you what, I made a great penfriend.

Crocodile Night Adventure

For a bloke who grew up never having much to do with the water, I always seem to be getting jobs either on the sea or up a river. My childhood was spent in the desert and no matter how hard I try, floating around just doesn't feel normal. It's not a natural act.

But when he gets around the countryside with the arse out of his pants, constantly broke, a bloke can't be too fussy what employment he gets. As long as there's a feed involved and the prospect of a few beers I'll usually do pretty well anything. **'Great Opportunity'** the advertisement read, standing out in bold print on the Katherine notice-board. It caught my eye as I was heading past on a mission to Kirby's back bar. I could do with a great opportunity so I read on: 'Tour guide with knowledge of crocodiles required for boat cruise on the Katherine River, great lifestyle and excellent remuneration.'

'Experienced tour guide' — no worries there, I'd had my own tour business. OK, I went broke straight off, but I was experienced.

'Knowledge of crocodiles' — now let's see, I'd been stalked eleven times, attacked twice, chased through the long grass with one snapping at me arse four or five times, and with a hangover I sexed a 4-metre male and vomited. Anyone with half a brain could work out that all that added up to real knowledge.

The boat cruise operated from a picturesque little bush resort on the river, only about ten minutes from Katherine. The boss, Peter, was a good sort of bloke, friendly and straight up. I was honest with him at the interview. I told him I was the man, but I also pointed out I was no Captain Cook on the water, but he reckoned he could train me up as far as the boat-operating went. We got on pretty well and he said the job was mine if I wanted it. But he also pointed out it would be challenging and have the added responsibility of the safety of the thirty or forty people they got on the cruise every night.

'No worries there,' I said. 'Responsibility is my middle name, and unless a job is unbelievably challenging I don't even bother to turn up.'

Pete was convinced, so I moved into a small bungalow room at the back of the resort and the next day I was on the river getting a feel of the boat with the boss. The boat was a long flat-bottomed punt with seating for about forty people. It had two antique outboards on the back and a little console at the stern where you piloted the thing. The outboards looked like something from the Ming Dynasty. I would have liked to have got them carbon-dated. I'd say they were purchased from the same company that was responsible for discovering the wheel.

When Peter reversed the boat away from the landing the outboards smoked up, but he reckoned they were pretty reliable and we cruised off down the river.

He took me up and down the 3 or 4 kilometre section used for the night cruise. The Katherine's a lovely river, with good clean flowing water. The banks are lined with large paperbarks and pandanus palms and white sandy beaches. In some sections it's pretty shallow and there were a few tricky parts, dodging sandbars and logs floating just under water level. There was also a set of rapids that took a bit of manoeuvring. Peter made it look pretty easy, but he pointed out that the boat, being a flat-bottomed job, didn't have a keel, so it was very touchy steering. One turn of the wheel and the arse-end would swing around, and if you didn't correct the steering a bit you found yourself spinning around and facing the opposite way.

I was out of control most of the day with Pete trying to tune me in. He had a lot of patience, that's for sure, but there was a hell of a lot to learn, especially the safety factor. All jokes aside, no tourist wants to get killed on a boat cruise. Safety was the big one. 'Bring 'em back in one piece,' Pete said. 'Nothing else matters, as long as they don't hurt themselves.'

I don't know why, but Pete had faith in me. That night a local women's club had booked the boat so me and Pete teamed up, and he said it was a good opportunity to see how things were done.

They rocked up pissed and she was a radical old cruise, with Pete nearly crashing the boat owing to the fact that four quite elderly women were trying to grab his old fella while he was at the helm. Fortunately, he only lost control of the vessel for a short time. I was at the front of the boat playing a song on the guitar and had my shorts pulled down in mid-strum. It was embarrassing because I had no jocks on. I went back to serving everyone wine, thinking, this boat cruise stuff is serious business. The women's club said they didn't get out much, so when they do, it can get a little festive.

We cruised down to a pretty little sandy beach and Pete brought the boat in. This was what they called the 'meal spot', so everyone got off the boat and Pete got a fire going and placed a big pot of stew near it to warm up.

The big attraction for the night was the crocodile feeding. Pete made a tapping noise on the side of a bucket with a stick and next minute about five crocs poked their head up out the water just in front of the bank. The women's club thought this was terrific and they started hooting and squealing. Then Pete gave the bucket another tap and the crocs came marching out the water and up on the sand.

This thinned the women's club out a bit, they were side-stepping all over the place. One lady who had just ducked into the shadows to take a leak must have got a shock, because she came running past with her pants still down around her ankles. Pete gave the crocs a small bit of fish, and it was amazing to see how relaxed they were, even with a screaming women's club bolting around. They were freshwater crocodiles, ranging from 1.5 metres to 3 metres. The crocs seemed to enjoy the interaction and after the feed they all moved up to the fire and lay around getting warm. After a while everyone forgot about them and kept on drinking.

We had the stew, and then a mob of freshwater turtles turned up and a heap of catfish. They obviously knew the routine and Pete fed them the leftovers. It was a really good night and I could see this type of cruise had a lot of potential. The hardest bit was getting the women's club back on the boat. By now most of them were rotten. I had to carry a few of them — some of the ladies had just lain down in the sand and choked out.

Pete started up the old smokies and we cruised off. I played a few more songs on the guitar, but after my shorts got pulled off again I gave it away. I got the spotlight out and as Pete drove I spotlighted a few crocs on the bank and the odd barramundi swimming past. The women's club were a great bunch, typical Katherine people, a good honest mob out to have a good honest time. It took me and Pete a good half-hour to get everyone off the boat and into their waiting bus.

That was my initiation into Crocodile Night Adventures. Pete asked me what I thought of the cruise and I told him it was brilliant, but that I'd be wearing jocks next time. So we did a few more trips together and had a few more intensive training sessions on the river during the day. After a few weeks he reckoned I was ready to solo. Captain Phil O'Brien was about to take the wheel. I was issued with a name tag that read 'Captain' in bold print and Pete had organised a little Irish backpacker called Big Al to be my crew.

Big Al knew nothing about boats and even less about crocs, but I could see we would make a great team. We prepared the boat for our maiden voyage. We loaded up the stew and plenty of wine and some fish for the crocs. Big Al reminded me of one of those little statues people have in their garden and he had a huge deep Irish voice. It was so deep that things used to vibrate when he spoke.

About sunset all the passengers turned up, probably about thirty of them. I was nervous as shit and so was Big Al. We got everyone on the boat and I went through a few safety instructions.

We reversed away from the landing, the outboards smoked up beautifully and a few asthmatics had to go for the ventolin spray. 'Nothing like a bit of fresh river air', I said.

We cruised off down the river and everyone instantly unwound and started to enjoy the scenery, and for a brief moment I thought everything might work out all right — until I took the first bend. I turned the boat a bit sharp and before I knew it we'd spin around and were facing back up river. I covered myself by saying I'd seen a croc, and a few Germans took photos. We spin round a few more times and each time I made out I'd seen something. I think I was a bit tense, seeing it was my first trip, so I tried to relax a bit. It's only a fun cruise on the Katherine River, I told myself, so just take it easy.

So I took it easy, and coming around the next bend I clipped a huge paperbark overhanging the river. I only just grazed it, but it was enough to make one of the biggest, heaviest old branches break off, and with a crack it landed directly on the front row and crushed four teenage German tourists.

Big Al was first on the scene. He did the right thing and lifted the branch off the injured tourists, who were dazed and in shock. But because of the weight of the log Big Al couldn't quite get it over the rail and into the water. So in the half-dark there's Big Al's silhouette staggering from one side of the boat to the other wrestling with the huge branch. People at the back of the boat were pissing themselves laughing because from there it really did look comical, but as I got close to the front people were crying and wailing and wanting to know what the hell was going on. The Germans in the front row who'd copped the direct hit were not only concussed and shocked, they also had a fair few serious cuts and abrasions.

And so I made the big announcement: 'Sorry folks, have to cut the trip short tonight.' Then I jumped back on the wheel and headed straight back to the landing and organised to get the wounded to hospital. And I tell you what, hell hath no fury like the scorn of a paying customer.

It took most of next day to fill out the accident report because for any accident on the water, whether it's a punt on the Katherine River or an oil tanker that's dropped its guts on the Barrier Reef, you have to fill out the same standard form.

If me and Big Al were nervous on the first cruise, we were shitting hot coals for the second one. All the passengers turned up at sunset chafing at the bit for their big night cruise. I tried to stay composed and hid behind the badge that read 'Captain', but I'm thinking I should be wearing another badge underneath that says, 'Not a really good one'.

Big Al took comfort in the fact he didn't come from this country and no matter what happened, he could just take off. We smoked our way clear of the landing and went through the safety spiel. I added, 'If by chance a whopping big branch falls into the boat, don't panic.' They thought I was joking! The sun set as we slipped along the shadowy old Katherine. I spun out, but Lady

A crocodile relaxing by the campfire after some stew.

Luck was with us because there really was a croc on the bank and the passengers thought, geez, the captain's got good eyes to spot that croc and spin the boat around so quick. In fact, the captain was all set for a nervous breakdown, and so was the crew.

We made it to the sandy little beach called the mealspot. The crocs came up and we all had a feed of stew. I sang a few songs accompanied by Big Al playing a rubbish bin with a length of rope attached to a broomstick, a sort of bush bass. Big Al explained it was an instrument played by farmers in the fields of Ireland, and some punters believed him. Me and Big Al called ourselves The Emotions and we rattled off a few good tunes and the night was going great — crocs lying around next to the fire, The Emotions and all the passengers sipping wine under the stars!

Now next thing on the itinerary was the billy tea demonstration. It was the boss Pete's idea, to give the night that real Aussie flavour. I boiled up the billy and threw the tea leaves in and swung the billy around a few times to settle the leaves to the bottom. 'We'll just let that tea draw for a minute,' I said.

I turned around for a sec to talk to Big Al and a little kid grabbed the red-hot billy of tea and tried to swing it around. We hear an almighty scream and everyone looks around and there's this little kid, steam coming off his tee-shirt with a billy can on his head, looking like a miniature version of Ned Kelly. The kid was waving his arms frantically and stamping his feet and in a split second his parents grabbed him and got the billy can off his head, poor little bugger. He was pretty badly burnt, it was just like a bad dream gone wrong. We scrambled everyone back on the boat and I made the announcement: 'Sorry folks, have to cut the trip short tonight.'

I gunned it all the way back to the landing, the kid screaming in pain the whole way. We got the minibus that belonged to the resort and rushed him and his family down to Katherine hospital. They admitted the kid and gave him something to settle him down a bit and the good news was although he was badly scalded, it probably wouldn't scar.

Back at the resort Pete the boss wanted to know if we'd run over an albatross, because we weren't having 'much fucking luck', but he left it at that. Pete even helped with the accident report the next day. He was probably one of the fairest bosses I ever had.

So if me and Big Al had been nervous on the first cruise, and shitting hot coals for the second, you could have put a camp oven with a damper in it next to my arse for the third and it would have cooked in twenty minutes. Big Al wanted to head back to war-torn Northern Ireland, he reckoned it was less stressful back there, but I talked him into staying. He reckoned if not for The Emotions he would have pulled out.

Gingerly we went through the now lengthening safety rave as we reversed our way out of the wall of exhaust fumes and putted off down the river. Amazingly, over the next week we didn't have one major accident.

We had three minor accidents instead.

Coming into the meal spot I miscalculated my speed and instead of gently nosing the boat up on the sand, I hit it pretty hard. A few passengers got thrown out of their seats and some camera gear was damaged, but at least it wasn't a hospital job. Another night, coming back up the river I fell asleep at the wheel and drove straight past the landing. The passengers burred up a bit and I came good about 200 metres on. Because the river was narrow up there, I had to reverse all the way back and the old motors smoked up really bad and the passengers got a good lungful of carbon monoxide, but we got 'em back in one piece. And that's the main thing, although some of them dogged it a bit.

Another night, coming into the landing after a really nice trip I managed to clip a pandanus palm — it was no big deal, but an insect jumped off the pandanus palm straight into the ear of a female passenger. It didn't just buzz around by the earhole, no, it shot straight down into the eardrum and the lady went berserk.

She was clawing at her ear and blaming me, it was entirely my fault she reckoned. I tried to point out to her that no matter how hard I tried, I couldn't control the insect world. She just turned on me, but in her defence it must have been painful because she ended up going to the hospital and had to get it surgically removed. It was right down in the workings of her inner ear, poor thing.

Me and Big Al both reckoned we were just having a bad run. We were really giving it our best shot. Statistically speaking, we were due for some luck. You can have a few accidents some of the time, but you can't have a lot of accidents all of the time. It doesn't make statistical sense. It's unstatistical. So me and Big Al, believing our run of bad luck was behind us, dug deep and found a bit of confidence and cheered up a bit. The boss Pete still had faith in us, the hospital had heard all about us, and the Marine Branch of Transport and Works had a heap of paperwork from us. We were making a name for ourselves. Optimism could and would prevail, I told Big Al.

And it did. The next two weeks were a breeze — beautiful dry-season weather, great nights on the river and some terrific people. A woman had a serious asthma attack one night and needed to get to hospital pretty quickly, and an old lady booted a croc fair in the guts because she thought it wasn't a real one, but thank God the thing just took off into the river. But on the whole things were panning out nicely and it looked like we'd weathered the storm. I even fell a bit in love one night, but she got that pissed she passed out not long after the cruise finished and her friends had to take her home. It was bad luck because I'm sure there was some electricity in the air, but I had to laugh, because it's usually me pulling that stunt.

Not long after that bit of failed romance, I had another funny experience. The boss Pete asked me if I could take the shuttle bus and drop two tourists into Katherine one night. He would have done it himself but he was too flat out. I didn't mind, especially when I saw them. One looked like Elle McPherson and the other looked like Linda Lovelace. We started chatting and on the way into town they noticed the turn-off to Katherine Hot Springs. 'What's that place like?' they asked, so I shot down there in the shuttle bus and thought I'd give them a quick look. It was late and the place was deserted so I grabbed the torch and we walked down the steps to the Springs. 'Oh, it's beautiful,' they said. 'Could you just hold the torch for us while we have a dip?'

Next minute they strip off completely and jump in and start splashing around and there's me holding the torch for them.

One of the girls winked at the other and said, 'At least we'll have something to hang our towel on.'

The boss Pete thought I was a great bloke when I told him I'd drive the shuttle bus any time he liked, and don't worry about paying me either, I said.

I was really settling into this boat cruise job. There wasn't a dull moment, that's for sure. Big Al was starting to enjoy himself as well. He still knew nothing about boats and crocs but his bush bass-playing was getting really good. Although we'd maimed and nearly killed a few tourists, our impromptu jam sessions down at the meal spot went over really well, and the gang of freshwater crocs that turned up every night made for a memorable time. On the nights when there wasn't an accident, it was a real bloody good little cruise.

But there's two things you can count on in life: dying and change.

And so it came to pass that Big Al's visa had all but run out and it was time for the Irish Crocodile Dundee to leave. I would miss him because in a short space of time we'd been through a lot.

So I lost my crew, but boss Pete said there were only ten people booked that night, so I could probably handle it myself. I was thinking it wouldn't be the same down at the meal spot without Big Al on the bush bass, but I didn't have to worry because I never made it that far. Shortly after we pulled away from the landing, I hit a slightly submerged log that was floating around.

The boat jerked to a sudden stop. Unfortunately, there was a lady up at the front of the boat holding a spotlight, scanning the river looking for crocs, as Big Al used to do. When the boat hit the log she was catapulted right off the front of the boat, flew through the air, did at least three big somersaults, levelled out and then piked straight into the river. She was a beefy lady and to her credit, when we fished her out she still had hold of the spotlight. She was half-drowned, terrified, in shock and badly injured, but she never let go of the spotty and I think that shows good qualities in a person.

An overweight guy was rolling around in the aisle between the seats, wheezing and groaning and clutching at his chest. He'd been taking photos at the time and when we hit the log he'd smashed into the seat in front of him, but although it looked bad he was just winded. His camera was in about eighteen different pieces.

I had to make the announcement: 'Sorry folks, have to cut the trip short tonight.' It was another dash to the hospital — by now I was on a first-name basis with most of the staff there. The lady with the spotty ended up spending ten days in hospital, but the bloke went home with a few bruised ribs. Next day at the filling out of the accident report ceremony, me and Pete had a bit of a talk and it was suggested I hand in my Captain's badge. I was to be de-commissioned. Or to put it in layman's terms, given the 'Royal Order of the Arse'.

Pete was a great boss, he had more than his fair share of patience and he'd given me every chance in the world, but a bloke like me just ain't cut out for the water. Give me the desert any time. Pete still wasn't convinced I hadn't killed an albatross somewhere along the line — maybe I had but if so I'd forgotten.

The Crocodile Night Adventure is a great night out if you're ever in the Katherine area. These days it's a totally professional operation and I can thoroughly recommend it. You won't strike blokes like me or Big Al on the boat, that's for sure. But I have been known to call in for a beer from time to time and take in the atmosphere of the lovely, untamed Katherine River, walk its banks and reminisce about yet another fantastic adventure . . . that got me absolutely nowhere.

The Campfire Singer

Music has always been a passion for me, no doubt about it. I picked up the guitar as a kid and learnt a few chords, and as the years went on I suppose I developed my own style. I've written a few songs about different places and people, but mostly they're about emotional things, for example, women that have dumped me. Pure poetry. Vocally I have been described as Jimmy Hendrix on half a lung, but as good as I was, I never really got anywhere. Getting pissed and singing around the campfire was my only claim to fame.

It was beautiful to see how I could work a drunken campfire crowd. I'd bring them up with an uplifting version of 'You Only Live Once, Then You Are Dead For A Long Time' (one I wrote based on fact), then I'd take them down to the emotional basement with a devastatingly tear-jerking version of 'Island Girl'. Usually I'd be half shot, perched on an esky, singing my heart out. It might be a stock camp or a bunch of tourists or just mates, but I always seemed to be the one entertaining.

When I was in full flight I could do no wrong. Like the time up at Kakadu, when I was singing a deep-and-meaningful to a bunch of Germans around a campfire and, unbeknown to me, my left ball was hanging out the side of my shorts. I couldn't work out why everyone was staring — I thought they were checking out the painting on my guitar. Some of the women looked pretty horrified. And I'm thinking, shit, I know it's a sad song but it's not that bad. Then the penny dropped. I looked down and saw one plum hanging out, so I casually finished the song and said, 'It's an old tradition, folks. In Australia, we always sit around the campfire with one ball hanging out.' And you know, they almost believed me. You see, when you have the crowd in the palm of your hand, you can get away with stuff like that.

Whichever way you look at it, in all modesty I was a very polished performer. Where does a bloke go to once he's reached the top of the heap? Let's face it, I'd written ten songs and I knew another two, so that made twelve songs. Creatively speaking, I was blossoming.

Now you wouldn't read about it, but three twists of fate took place around that time, events that would lead me to my musical destiny.

The first twist of fate was that floating log on the Katherine River when I was working as boat driver for the Crocodile Night Adventure Cruise company — the one that caused a female tourist to be catapulted out of the boat and into the murky depths.

The second happened after I'd filled out an incredibly long accident report the next day. I flicked through the local paper and there it was, shining like a beacon in the job vacancies section: 'Singer/Guitar Player Wanted in Outback Resort'.

And the third was getting the arse from Crocodile Night Adventure Cruises. Now tell me that wasn't fate. Without a doubt, I was being guided by a higher force.

So on the phone I hopped. I got straight onto the manager of the resort and, like any decent young Australian, I was prepared to spin any amount of bullshit to secure the job.

The resort manager proceeded to fire a few questions at me. I pretty well had them covered, and when I told him I'd just returned from a tour in Memphis he really started to get interested. I told him I knew all the oldies as well as the newies, and was willing to bend over backwards and sing them directly out my arse if need be. He said that probably wouldn't be necessary, but he liked my enthusiasm and I got the job.

So I packed the old Toyota for the trip and headed off. I planned on two to three days' travelling, taking into account pubs along the way. I threw in a few extra flash shirts, you know, a couple of frilly rhinestone jobs for the gig, and I brushed the cobwebs off an old pack of condoms, just in case the impossible happened, and blew out of Katherine trying to remember the words to an old Creedence song.

There's nothing like the open road to unwind and do a bit of thinking. As usual I saw the romantic side of things as opposed to the more realistic. I had visions of sipping cold beer by the resort pool in the day, and at night getting standing ovations for my twelve fantastic songs. I only had just enough money to get there, so if it didn't work out I was stuffed. But being the total optimist I am, thoughts of failure didn't enter my head.

Phil at his campfire,
thankfully not wearing shorts.

The old Toyota purred along the Stuart Highway, reliable as ever. Shame the rego had run out, but you can't win them all, I'm thinking, as I swerved to miss a wedge-tail eagle chewing on a bit of wallaby schnitzel squashed on the road. I was ready to root, shoot and electrocute, ready to pour my heart out in song, ready to devastate audiences with my charm.

I strode into the reception area of the resort, a jukebox on legs, looking for the manager. A nice little girl at the counter asked me if I'd like to book a room for the night, but I said, 'She's right, I'm the new musician, gunna do a bit of playing.' She did a double-take and looked at me in disbelief. I said, 'Hey baby, I don't look like much but wait till I croon.' She went red and slinked away. What did she expect, bloody Elvis?

The manager finally showed up. He was a dark skinny little bloke of about five foot two and reminded me of Barney Rubble from 'The Flintstones'. The duty manager was with him. He was deeply tanned and had a sharp look about him, similar to the wedge-tail I nearly ran over on the way down.

They both looked me up and down as if I was the dingo that took Lindy Chamberlain's baby, and I was starting to think I might be a late scratching. I obviously wasn't what they expected, but we went through the motions. They showed me my room, which was pretty good, and gave me a book of rules and regulations whilst working at the resort. It was crammed with all sorts of laws and codes of behaviour, not what you'd describe as a little light reading. I hung my rhinestone numbers on a coat-hanger and went for a walk to check things out.

The resort was split into two sections. One section had a campground and budget dormitories with a cafe and small bar. Plenty of people were milling around. This area was obviously for the backpackers and caravanners. The other section was more exclusive, with luxurious motel rooms, a fantastic restaurant and balcony area, a pool and nice bar. Both sections had great views out across the country. The colours and general feeling of this area were tremendous, so much spirit.

The next morning I was up with the sun, ready to create musical history. The butcher birds were going their hardest at first light outside my room, giving it heaps with their throaty little tunes. I checked out the rules book and turned to the chapter concerning staff breakfasts. I moved off in the appropriate manner, walked to the appropriate eating area, appropriately ordered an appropriate staff breakfast and, in the manner appropriate to a staff member, I ate. All these rules were already giving me the shits; it made a bloke feel like he was back at school.

After breakfast, I figured it was time to chew the fat with Barney Rubble about my musical destiny. As it turned out he wanted me to kick off that night on the balcony up at the flash restaurant. There was a little stage set up and a sound system all ready to go. I jokingly said to Barney, 'The girls better hold onto their pants, because when I start strumming emotions go wild.' Barney Rubble looked at me as if I was a complete imbecile. It was like I was speaking in a foreign language.

Later that night I rocked up at the flash restaurant, ready to kick off a startling new career in music. Half of me was excited, the other half (probably the half with the brain) was thinking, what the hell have I got myself into now?

The restaurant was pretty busy, probably over a hundred punters, all stylish types, some real knock-outs just quietly. Out on the balcony there were a fair few people sitting around, sipping champers and watching the sunset. Some had already put the nosebag on.

Well, I thought, no time like the present — time to plug in and pour it out, time to slay them with the big twelve. So up to the stage I went, which, by the way, was two old pallets with a bit of carpet thrown on top that smelt like tomcat piss. They really outdid themselves with the stage. The sound system looked like something they'd stolen from Cash Converters, but I plugged the old girl in and adjusted a few knobs and, to my surprise, the thing arced up, so I gave the guitar a couple of strums and it didn't sound half bad. Then I did a quick test with the mike, and I was ready to fire.

At that moment I would have paid big money for a shot or two of rum just to settle me down a bit, but without further ado I said into the microphone, 'Gidday, folks, my name's Phil O'Brien, has anyone been to India? Well, get this one inderya.'

Off I went, strumming the guts out of the guitar and singing my hardest. I reckon I sounded not bad at all, somewhere between Willie Nelson and Reg Lindsay. I was really crooning it out, and as I finished off the first song I half expected a clap or two or at least a nod of a head. But there was nothing. No one even looked up. So I said into the microphone, just to stir them up a bit, 'Thanks, folks, that was one I wrote back in Memphis with the King.' Still nothing. So off I went into song two, an emotional number about how women use me for my body. I finished that one and said, 'Thanks, folks, that one's doing big things for me in Zimbabwe.' Still nothing.

So on I ploughed, song three, a tune about a German girl who dumped me, called 'Waltzing Von Hilda'. Still nothing. So I sang a couple more and then announced that I'd just take a short break. 'You've been a great audience,' I said. No one gave a shit. I'm thinking, either none of this mob speaks English or they just couldn't give a hoot. I think I was pretty right on both counts.

As I walked up to the bar, I noticed most of the people were European, mainly German by the sound of things, with a sprinkling of Japanese and bugger-all Australians — they probably couldn't afford the joint. Most of the punters were really tucking into the tucker as well, probably hungry after hiking around all day, so no need to take it too bad, I'm thinking. My next bracket might get a better response. A cold beer would pick me up no doubt. So up to the bar I went, only to find staff weren't allowed to drink whilst on duty. Well, that was a piece of tragic news and if I wasn't depressed before, I was now! But into it I went again, song after song. The only response I got this time was when some old bloke walking past flicked twenty cents into my guitar case. I didn't know whether to laugh or cry or get up and snot him.

The one positive thing about playing at this restaurant was that I could sing pretty well anything. For example, I could play the same song a couple of times, or even just make one up as I went along, or sing the same verse over and over to kill a bit of time. As no one spoke English and no one gave a stuff, I could get away with anything. Of course I got the odd look from some of the staff at times, but they'd get over it. Every now and then I'd con some German into getting me a beer and I'd go and drink it out in the carpark, away from the other staff.

Musically I think I was going pretty good, and after a few weeks I was kind of enjoying the experience. Unfortunately my love life still hadn't ignited and this was causing me concern. Night after night incredibly beautiful women would file in and out of the joint, but as far as they were concerned I was just someone making noise in the corner. But as bad as things get you should never forget one thing: every dog has his day. Well, he's meant to anyway.

Mine came on a Saturday night. I remember the day because the night before was Friday the thirteenth, and a plague of giant beetles came through the resort. I was playing out on the balcony at the time. Beetles were everywhere doing the big kamikaze, so all the punters moved inside and the staff shut the big glass doors. That was quite OK, except for the fact they locked me out there playing to no one, and everyone inside the restaurant was looking out at me on the balcony like I was a nut. I was covered in beetles and so pissed off that I just carried on regardless.

When Saturday night came, everyone was back on the balcony again and the beetles had moved on to wherever beetles move on to. I was strumming away when all of a sudden my top lip started curling back a bit. Now this usually means only one thing. So I had a quick scan around and, sure enough, there she was, sitting just to the left of my intricate stage set-up, on her lonesome. She definitely had all the right stuff in all the right places, but for some reason she looked down in the dumps, like someone had just run over her dog or something.

Now it had been quite a while between drinks for the old campfire singer, but the senses were still very finely tuned. She had boyfriend trouble written all over her face. Without a doubt a very vulnerable time for any impressionable young woman. I thought I'd strum a sad one and see how she took it.

She took it rough. She slumped down on the table, head in her hands. I'm thinking, this girl needs help, so I played an uplifting one, but it didn't seem to work. I think she was still too affected from the sad one I'd played before and she was going down fast. Any minute it looked like she was going to drop down on the ground and go into the foetal position.

Better do something, I'm thinking, so I announced to the Germans and Japanese, 'You've been great but I'm taking a short break,' and as usual they showed about as much emotion as a stack of fence posts lying at the railway station. I casually strolled over, the caring human being that I am, and asked her how she was going. I was half expecting her to tell me to get lost, but she looked up and gazed straight into my eyes, and for a minute there we were locked onto each other's gaze like a pair of heat-seeking missiles. I think she thought I was OK, which made me think she must be hard up, fed up or just plain washed up.

So we introduced ourselves, and I know it sounds ridiculous, but it was at that precise moment I realised I was a bit on the bugle. This was due to the fact that the last time I'd worn that shirt was about six months ago when I was working in a stock camp near Borroloola and I hadn't washed it since. She must have noticed the smell as well and said, 'Mmm, mmm, what's that aftershave you're wearing?'

'Ah,' I said, 'er, ah, it's a new one called, ah, it's called Brumby.'

'Mmm, very earthy,' she said.

Well, after that we just hit it off. As I'd predicted, she'd just busted up with a bloke down in Melbourne and she sounded like she was doing it tough, so I told her a couple of my hard-luck stories and it seemed to pick her up a bit. We decided that we both needed a little bit of an adventure, and I came up with the great idea of going for a swim in a lovely little spring nearby. I'd never swum in it before, but it looked really inviting, I told her.

So we left the roaring crowd to dribble into their buffet and took off. It was a beautiful steamy hot night, complete with wild lightning and the sound of thunder rolling across the flat. It was as if nature had choreographed a perfect scenario for romance. I felt pretty sure I'd be climbing into the saddle at some stage of the night, no worries at all.

We got to the spring and peeled the gear off and jumped in. The atmosphere was incredible and pretty soon we were kissing and steaming up the spring, so I thought I'd get the momentum going a little more and give her a bit of the old caress. So I ran my hand gently down her thigh and I felt all these rubbery lumpy things all over her and I'm thinking, what's the go here? Then it hit me — *leeches!* The spring was full of them. Unfortunately, I had to tell her that we'd better get out. It was a real shame because she was getting up to maximum revs and I'm sure we were just about to consummate our relationship.

When we got out and when she saw the leeches she chucked a wobbly, I mean she really lost it. I tried to get them off her as quickly as I could, blood going everywhere. Of course it looked worse than it was. If you get them off quickly, it's not really a problem, but I couldn't get that through to her. She was going hysterical, screaming and stuff. She wound herself up so much she started to hyperventilate, so I slapped her gently to try to snap her out of it. Then she slapped me about seventeen times harder, grabbed her gear and stormed off.

I'm thinking, every dog has his day. But not this one!

Next night, I'm back on the balcony trying to put the trauma of the previous night behind me. Feeling a little emotional, I got an idea for a new song. I was going call it

'The Lord Giveth and the Lord Taketh Away'. So I strummed out what was in my head and, as usual, the Germans and Japanese just grazed on. Then, out of the blue, in raced Barney Rubble and the duty manager. They came up to me in a fairly urgent manner and announced that a group over in the corner, who were doing a tour with the bus company Australian Pacific, wanted me to come over and lead them in a rousing 'Happy Birthday, Australian Pacific', as it was the bus company's seventieth year of service. I thought for a minute then said, 'Look, mate, I'd do just about anything to help anyone, but I take my music pretty serious and I'll be buggered if I'm singing "Happy Birthday" to a bus.'

Barney's bottom lip dropped and the look on his face reminded me of someone who'd just lost everything in a bush fire. The duty manager on the other hand looked as if he was ready to clip two electrodes to my testicles and hit the switch. They both spun on their heels and took off, and I realised I'd lost a lot of popularity over that one, but bugger 'em, I'm a serious artist, so I went back to singing 'The Lord Giveth and the Lord Taketh Away', the story of a young bloke who misses out on love because of a violent leech attack. A very sad little tune.

The next night up on the balcony the most amazing thing happened. One of the punters came up and actually talked to me. He was a young German and his English wasn't real good but he wanted to know if I could cook a damper. I told him I'd knocked out a few in my day and he asked if I could show him how, so we arranged to meet the next day.

He wasn't a bad sort of bloke, and when we met he had an esky full of cold cans — he showed a lot of initiative for a German. We took off in my old Toyota, I found a bit of good wood and proceeded to show him the ins and outs of damper creation. We had a great day drinking an enormous amount of cold beer under a particularly hot sun, and in the end rolled out a nice damper.

When we finally got back to the resort I was fairly lubricated. The German bloke had pretty well run his race and the last I saw of him, he was staggering off with the damper tucked under his arm. As I'd hardly eaten all day, I was thinking a rum or two would be nice. I wandered into the little bar at the resort — no problem, as I was off duty and it was legal to have a drink. I thought I was moving pretty well for a bloke who'd been drinking all day and was feeling really happy with myself.

The bar manager, who was built like a Canadian brown bear, gave me the once-over and scowled. Although he had nothing on me, I could see he didn't like me much. I don't really know why, but he was wound up tight, that was for sure. I managed to get a rum out of him and then I started chatting with two extremely charming girls at the bar. Being five-eighths pissed, I was full of bravado and told the girls all sorts of bullshit. They were enjoying themselves and we had a good old time. My excitement was short-lived because they announced to me they were lesbians, but we continued enjoying chatting.

It must have been too much for the performing Canadian brown bear bar manager — the three of us having a good time at the bar was really burning him up. He came over and fronted me, and demanded that I get out of the bar. No pleasantries or reasons, just 'GET OUT', as if he was talking to someone's mongrel dog.

Well, the old adage 'the bigger they are the harder you fall' doesn't really apply when you've had a tank full, and although I'm a peace-loving person I wasn't going to stand for these stand-over tactics, so I tried to grab him and give him one. He'd really got my goat and I was going to punch him somewhere into next fortnight.

Some German backpackers jumped on me and tried to stop me, which was fair enough — they were just trying to defuse the situation. The bear picked up the phone to ring the boss, so I grabbed the phone out of his hands and speared it straight at his head. He ducked and the phone smashed against the wall, exploding into several pieces. I said, 'Ring him now, see if he's home.' He was fairly stunned, so I took the opportunity to stand back and gloat.

The moment was short-lived, because little did I know his wife was in an office at the side of the bar and she'd rung the boss. Before I knew it, there was Barney Rubble in his pyjamas, standing right next to me. The show was over. He wanted me in the office first thing in the morning. I left the bar peacefully, as I really don't like violence, but I suppose everyone's got limits to what they'll put up with.

The next morning I went to the office with a hangover that would have registered on the Richter scale. There was me, Barney Rubble and the duty manager. I'm sure they would have loved to stake me out over an ants' nest.

Barney said, 'You've damaged resort equipment, I'm going to have to terminate your contract.' Then he added, 'You also refused to sing "Happy Birthday" to Australian Pacific and I'm sure you weren't going to sing

"Jingle Bells" at Christmas and no doubt you would refuse to sing "Auld Lang Syne" on New Year's Eve.'

'Mate,' I said, 'I think you've got me on that one.' How can you argue with that logic? This was no place for a bloke with my artistic capabilities, so I got up, packed up and pissed off.

The last I saw of that resort and my musical destiny was in my rear-vision mirror, slowly disappearing. An hour or so down the road, I stopped to boil the billy and make some coffee as the hangover was getting the better of me. I lit a fire and got some water going, then plucked out my guitar and had a bit of a strum. Through my hangover haze I realised one thing: the old campfire singer was back where he belonged . . . just singing around the campfire!

Powelly's Last Ride

It was *getting tough* on the old croc farm, pet-meat prices were moving higher and higher, and the crocs seemed to be eating more and more. Things were starting to look a little tight. All the hatchlings, the saleable items, were growing out really well, but they weren't quite ready to sell just yet. So cash flow was on the lean side. I figured it might be a good idea to do a bit of hunting and try and save the farm some money.

I wanted to target water buffalo, as they weigh in at over a tonne and that meant a lot of meat for the farm. Roos and feral pigs weren't much good — too much effort for not a lot of return.

Water buffalo aren't native to Australia. They were introduced back in the late 1800s, but they adapted so well they reached plague proportions, causing enormous erosion and damage to the wetland areas of the Top End of the Territory. So the government launched a huge eradication program in the 1980s to try and wipe them out. They were almost successful, but there were still areas where buff could be found.

Unfortunately, the Aboriginal workforce on the farm was away, as there was a big ceremony on, and I didn't know when they'd be back. I needed help, so I thought it was a good idea to visit an old friend of mine, Colin Powell.

Powelly was a part-Aboriginal bloke in his fifties, a top bushman. His skill with a butcher's knife was legendary and he was a good bloke to have around. These days he lived a relatively quiet existence, but in his early days I think he played it pretty hard. One time a few years back he rattled someone's cage a bit too hard. I don't know the exact circumstances, but Powelly got shot twice in the stomach at point-blank range. Somehow he survived it. He always joked that before he got shot he had a serious diabetes problem, but after he got his pancreas blown out it wasn't a problem anymore. He was a happy-go-lucky kind of bloke and I really liked him.

I drove down to his camp in the early morning. Powelly had just finished breakfast which that day consisted of a six-pack of beer and one half-roasted echidna. A true breakfast of champions! Iron-man stuff. The only thing Powelly liked better than echidna was tongue. He loved tongue — bullock tongue, buffalo tongue, any tongue. He'd boil it up and slice into it like cheese. Better than chocolate, he reckoned. A cold beer and a slice of tongue and Powelly was happy. He was in his twilight years and was really enjoying the finer things in life.

Powelly had some good ideas about where I might find a mob of buffalo, and with a little luck he reckoned we just might get a few in the freezer. The place he suggested was about seven or eight hours' drive away, out towards an open coastal plain, a fair hike. As I'd hoped, Powelly was dying to come along as well. He reckoned he hadn't had a good feed of tongue for ages. And someone better come and show the young bloke how to do it.

Out of respect, the old Aboriginal bloke who was the elder for that area was notified. He was only too happy to give his permission, especially once he knew old Powelly would be coming out. The only condition was to drop him and his family off some meat if we got lucky. Next move, a couple more blokes, a couple of rifles, a trailer, some diesel, and no self-respecting buffalo in East Arnhemland would be safe.

The first friend I called on was Tony Pierce, one of my close friends, a middle-aged bloke who ran the local slipway where he did repairs on boats. Tony was a real Errol Flynn-style character. Nothing fazed him and he was only too happy to come and help knock a few buff over for the croc farm. He thought it might be a good chance to bring his son Jimmy on a little adventure, show him a few of the old man's tricks.

Setting out: from left to right, Jimmy, Old Powelly, Mark Johnson and me.

Mark Johnson was the next mate I grabbed, an easy-going bloke, very resilient. Mark only had to eat every second or third day and, like the drover's dog, was all prick and ribs.

So all up she was a pretty star-studded line-up.

Together we managed to scrape up an old World War Two .303 rifle off some old digger and one .22 Magnum. The .22 would have been great for rabbits but no way would it ever stop a buffalo, but we brought it anyway so as not to offend the old bloke that lent it to us. Next morning we met at the croc farm and it reminded me of that line from the famous poem 'The Man from Snowy River', the bit that reads: 'All the cracks had gathered to the fray'.

Everyone was hungover after a blinder at the local club the night before and I almost called it off, but the meat situation was desperate. Powelly hadn't fronted, so we drove down to his camp and found him still a little under the weather from last night, but his enthusiasm was undaunted. So we loaded him into the back of the Toyota and hit the track. Me and Jimmy in the front, with Tony, Mark and old Powelly flaked out in the tray.

It really wasn't the perfect way to start a serious hunting expedition I was thinking. One bloke was already passed out, and the others weren't far off. We weren't exactly what you'd call a picture of health.

After a few hours on the Central Arnhem Highway, which is just a dirt road with a big name, we turned off onto a little goat-track which we hoped would take us out to the country Powelly was talking about. It was a slow trip through creeks and washaways, and up and down rocky hills and gullies. The hangover heads in the back were starting to call out for a hair of the dog, so we had a bit of a blow in the shade alongside a pretty little creek and all relaxed with a cold beer.

The Crack Buff Hunting Outfit wasn't looking real flash at that stage. After smoko we crossed the creek and pushed on, the track petering out until there wasn't one. Through the bush we poked and, as Powelly predicted, the country started to open up and just as the sun was setting we found ourselves on some promising-looking open plains country.

A bit of buff shit was dotted around the place and the odd track or two, so the signs looked good. The Crack Buff Hunting Party had got over their hangovers by now and were slipping into the beer a bit, but I was confident everyone could still handle themselves. It may have looked like we were driving around in circles, stopping every two minutes for someone to have a leak, but in fact we were like a venomous snake, just waiting to strike!

When the sun was well and truly down the blokes on the back arced up the spotlight. Around we went, spotlight sweeping, following tracks and keeping a sharp eye out, senses finely tuned. Powelly, who by now had repositioned himself in the front seat, was sound asleep and snoring away like a chainsaw in need of a tune-up. Jimmy was nodding off, and there wasn't much noise coming from the back either.

Then presto! One buff caught in the beam of the spotlight, totally mesmerised, about 100 metres away.

'Righto, Tony, Mark, go for it! Buff! There! Go for it,' I commanded.

Nothing happened, then Powelly woke up and instinctively screamed out, 'Shoot the bastard!'

At last, action on the back of the Toyota — clang, clang, beer cans kicked out the way, bullets being dropped by shaky hands. The boys on the back weren't real slick. Finally someone gets a shot away but the buff's long gone by now.

We wouldn't have won any gold medals for that performance. Powelly dropped back to sleep and started snoring again. At that stage it didn't look like we would pose any threat to the buffalo community of Arnhemland. Time for a bit of a meeting.

We all got out, except for Powelly, and had a bit of a walk around and splashed a bit of water on our faces, had a leak, and did a bit of soul-searching. We psyched ourselves up for a better effort next time. I pointed out it had been a great trip getting out there but now we had to make things worthwhile.

The Crack Squad agreed. So off we poked, this time in a much more alert state . . . well, at least everyone was awake this time! Even old Powelly fired up a bit.

We scanned and scanned with the spotlight then bingo! Two shapes moving across the flat up in front of us. Kaboom went the fire-power from the back of the Toyota, kaboom, and the two shapes kept hopping out across the flat. It was two kangaroos, but it didn't matter, we'd missed them anyway.

An hour later, with Powelly snoring again, I was just beginning to think we weren't going to do much good, when coming around a bend we hit the jackpot — about six or seven buff out on the flat. I booted the Toyota and raced off across the flat. I wanted to get around them and work them into a bunch. Then I figured we might have a chance of getting the lot.

Easier said than done. The buff were up and running but we were gaining. The ground was rough and bumpy and the blokes on the back were hanging on for dear life, but no one had started to abuse me yet so I knew everything was all right. Across the flat we roared in the old Toyota and finally caught the mob. I swung out wide around them pushing them into a small group.

Powelly woke up, took in the whole scene instantly and issued the command: 'Shoot the bastard!'

The boys started shooting and I kept driving in large circles around the buffalo keeping them together. The crack shots on the back were going their hardest but it's never easy shooting from a moving vehicle and it was pretty rough country.

The buff decided it was time to make a break for it. At this stage we'd dropped a couple and wounded a couple and about three galloped off, so we took after them and managed to pull alongside one and shoot it. Then we tried it with another one and somehow Tony missed and managed to shoot the indicator light off the Toyota!

I thought we should steady up for a bit, so we went back and put the two wounded ones out of their misery. That was five and we figured that would do us. The plan was to get stuck into it at first light, cut them up and try to get the meat back to the croc farm freezer before it went off.

The Crack Buff Hunting Outfit was now starting to tire a bit. It had been a big day and we'd done pretty well, considering it only took about three hundred and twenty-seven bullets to get five buffalo. At least there'd be plenty of meat for the croc farm. Time to roll out the swag and rest up for the morning. We lit a good fire and camped on the plain.

As I was lying in my swag that night I had a little laugh to myself. It was ironic — not all that far away from where we were was one of those safari-type camps where big-game hunters fly out from the USA and pay thousands of dollars to nail a buff. Shit, I'm thinking, a couple of them could have come with us for nothing. They would've had more fun anyway. I couldn't really work out why people pay all that money to kill animals. Personally I hate killing anything, but the old buffalo causes a lot of damage and it's a feral animal, and this time the meat was for a good cause.

First light came around pretty quick, as it usually does when you're really stuffed, and the Crack Unit was a bit sluggish getting out of their swags, but after a billy of tea and a bit of steak it started to step pretty lively. It would take a big effort to get these buff cut up. We knew we had to really move it, as the weather was pretty warm and humid, just the right conditions for sending meat off in a hurry.

Powelly was an absolute artist with a knife. He dabbed and poked and sliced like a real Picasso, it was great to see him in action. With a knife in his hand, old Powelly was transformed; he wasn't Powelly anymore, he was Powelly van Gogh, ready to create another masterpiece.

He'd look at the buff from this angle, then from that angle, a slice here, a poke there, next minute the hindquarter's off; a lick with the steel, a dab, a thrust, then the shoulder's off; a quick jab or two and the tongue's out. A true artist.

We finished the first two, and by then the sun was up and it was getting warm so we started to rush the next couple. Powelly, as artistic as he was, was puffing out, so

Mark, me (with bandaged hand) and Powelly
skinning the buffalo.

I went at it a bit harder and made a slip and sliced the side of my hand open. It was a pretty bad cut, plenty of blood coming out, so I wrapped a rag around it. The bleeding eventually stopped, but it slowed me right down. Not long after that Tony stuck a knife fair in his leg just behind his knee, he'd somehow slipped and driven it right in. He went down big time. Apart from the bleeding he went into a bit of shock as well, so we wrapped a blanket around him and laid him in the shade.

The Crack Buffalo Hunting Outfit was looking a little rag-tag, we were going down like ninepins, but we kept at it, the sun getting higher and higher. The trailer was finally loaded with the last hindquarter. Tony needed stitches pretty badly so we wasted no time and headed off, Powelly complaining he'd never had time to boil a tongue up!

It was a slow trip back, with the trailer full of buff meat, poor Tony wrapped in a blanket bouncing around on the back, Powelly craving a cold beer and a hot tongue, and me trying to negotiate the goat-track towing three or four tonnes and with a hand that didn't want to stop bleeding. It was a real slog.

We stopped in as we'd promised to the Aboriginal elder's camp and dropped off a hindquarter. Old Powelly and he chatted in Aboriginal, and I'm pretty sure something was said about hunting buffalo with amateurs. But they both nearly pissed themselves laughing.

We got back to town well into the night sometime. The morale of the Crack Buff Squad had deteriorated slightly after the eight-hour trip. Everyone, including me, was absolutely stuffed. We pulled into the hospital and I'll be buggered — in an ironic twist of fate, there's a water buffalo feeding on the lawn just out the front of Emergency! We were so stunned, no one had the energy

Heading home — Powelly, Tony (injured and wrapped in a blanket), me and Mark.

even to throw a rock at it. We just staggered past in single file into the hospital.

After everyone got stitched up, I dropped Powelly and his bag of tongues off. He wasn't feeling too crash-hot. I thanked him for his help and he wandered off to his camp, tired but happy. He'd had the chance to get out there and do a bit of hunting again.

No one knew that this was to be Powelly's last trip. A little later down the track Powelly passed away and the Northern Territory lost one of its great bush characters. A hard life had finally caught up with him. There were no frills with Powelly. He was what he was, a bushman and a survivor and he cut his own track through life. He was good to be around, and although he was a bloke who never really had much, nothing stopped him sharing what he did have.

As a show of respect for Powelly we all agreed that if we ever see that buffalo on the lawn of the hospital again, we'll knock it over and bone it out right there on the spot, just for old times' sake. He would have liked that.

Places, Pubs and People

Sometimes I wish I had a dollar for every interesting character I've met in a bush pub. I reckon I'd be rollin' in it. I've seen all sorts of sights over the years wandering around the country, some of them pretty rugged, even with my low standards of behaviour.

I've seen blokes stand on their head and try and skull yard glasses — with no trousers on. And feats of amazing strength, like the dwarf that climbed onto a bar-stool, tapped this big bloke on the shoulder and then knocked him out. I think there was a girl involved, but the little bloke really showed spirit.

But one bloke I'll never forget was a gnarly wrinkled-up old Thursday Islander who used to drift into this pub from time to time. The only thing I ever heard him say was 'Number Nine'. That was it! He'd either sidle up next to you at the bar and say 'Number Nine', or else he'd come in and rip out some really loud bird-call, then everyone would turn around to see what was going on. There would be the old bloke and he'd just say 'Number Nine'.

Another thing he used to do once he'd got everyone's attention was to light a match and then place it in between the wrinkles on his forehead. He'd put a cigarette in his mouth and with his lips, using no hands, he'd somehow point the cigarette up to the lit match wedged between the wrinkles of his forehead and light it. Then still with no hands he'd take a few drags and swallow the cigarette. Of course by now everyone would be looking at him, so he'd make the announcement 'Number Nine'. Then he'd cough and next minute out of his mouth would come the lit cigarette still smoking and no one can believe it. Then he'd say very solemnly, 'Number Nine'.

Don't ask me why, but in his own way he was a likeable sort of bloke. You could talk to him all right, and he'd sit there and listen — you could talk about work or fishing or anything but the reply would always be the same, just 'Number Nine'. I never found out why — no one seemed to know — but he never upset anyone, he just did his thing.

You meet some really interesting people at pubs, and there's always a lot more to those establishments than first meets the eye. Without a doubt, pubs are the nerve centres of most country towns. That's where all the big decisions are made and most of the world's problems get solved there as well. Country romances generally begin at the pub, and usually end there, when one or the other never wants to go home. I also think group therapy originated in outback pubs, and someone's always got the answers.

When I'm looking for work I generally start at the pub, and I've had some good results over the years. Kalgoorlie in the Western Australian goldfields was a great place for pubs. There were pubs all over the place in that town — I think it worked out to about one pub per person. You only had to do a half-decent pub crawl and you'd always land some work, as well as a hangover. But the real jewel of the goldfields, the big attraction, was Hay Street.

For those readers not up to date with Australian geography, Hay Street in Kalgoorlie is the major stress-relief centre for the goldfields of Western Australia.

Girls of all shapes and sizes operate out of these corrugated-iron structures that resemble stables — although I think these days the premises might have been modernised and styled up a bit. The girls are genuinely lovely caring souls who provide a much-needed service for blokes who've been working out bush for weeks on end. They come into town a bit full around the cheeks and head straight down to Hay Street for a bit of attention.

I never actually went down there myself, but this was what I heard from other blokes.

The locals called the area 'the knockers', but the girls who worked down the knockers had a bit of class and they were pretty dedicated to the cause. Anyway, that's what I heard from other blokes, not actually going down there myself. I'd done a bit of time in the goldfields, generally working on drilling rigs for a while. It was a pretty carefree period of my life, working hard, saving absolutely nothing and relentlessly spending any money I made with no self-discipline at all.

Fairly similar to most other periods of my life.

But with all the jobs I've had and all the places I've wandered, it's always the people that make a place, and it's the interaction with different characters and the things you learn along the way that is money in the bank for me.

So anyway, to cut a long philosophical story short, working on a drilling rig out from Kalgoorlie got me absolutely nowhere. But I'll never forget the principles displayed by one girl working down at the knockers. This girl had style and she deservedly gained the respect of drilling crews from all corners of the goldfields.

The average stint on a drilling rig was about four to six weeks straight but one bloke I knew had done nine weeks. So when he hit town he headed straight down to Hay Street for the full service. The procedure once inside one of the knockers was the 'warm-water wash'. The girl would politely steer you to a basin full of warm water and you were asked to drop your block and tackle in it, and she'd then proceed to give it a going over with a bar of soap.

Well, this bloke who'd done nine weeks straight found it all too much, and from all reports he never even lasted the warm-water wash. Apparently a few rubs with the soap and it went off like an unattended fire hose. The girl promptly gave him his money back. That was the spirit of Hay Street — the spirit of Kalgoorlie.

Of course, all this information I got second-hand from the other blokes. I actually never went down there myself.

I don't know if you realise this, but towns that aren't fortunate enough to have a university usually have a good pub. The pub doubles as a place of learning and knowledge. Subjects are varied, but philosophy's always big, especially after a few cans on a hot day. And most bar staff specialise in marriage guidance as well.

Heartbreak Hotel down near Borroloola in the Northern Territory has really set some high standards in language studies, and the age-old art of fighting on the verandah is still practised there. I've studied at Heartbreak a few times although I never actually completed my last course. After I'd drunk an enormous amount of grog someone threw me in the back of a ute with a sober, highly refined, very sensitive female school teacher. As we left the pub at a fairly high speed I fell asleep. The driver ran over a kangaroo, stopped, threw it in the back of the ute and drove off again. I woke up face down in the ute with this warm body pressed up against my back. I thought it was the school teacher getting romantic. So I rolled over and sprang on top, ready to perform the act of love.

Everyone gets it wrong sometimes.

Whichever way you like to look at it, country pubs are Australian institutions of the highest order. Not only do they double as universities but they can also be spiritual places, places where visions are often experienced, and after eleven o'clock on most nights, it's not uncommon for men and women to speak in tongues.

Sometimes science just has no answers.

For example, 'time warp' is a phenomenon associated with outback pubs. Sometimes time stands still, and sometimes a pub seems to fall into some type of zone where time means nothing.

I got trapped in the zone once myself. On calling into Mary River Roadhouse one afternoon to make a phone call, I left four days later. It was all a complete blank and I still don't know what happened, but all my money was gone. It was a mystery.

Outback pubs have bred some resilient characters, there's no doubt about it. These characters are part of our country's soul and they've made us what we are as a country. It's from here that the spirit has been generated, the spirit that got us through world wars and put us on the map in sporting events. Their eccentricities and their will to overcome great odds have leached their way into Australian society and become the fuel that drives us on. It flows in our veins.

I can only thank my lucky stars that I've had the opportunity to live in and move around Australia's outback society, a place where freedom is the life's blood and a bloke feels as if he's got some identity. There's simple pleasures all around outback Australia, and they don't cost a thing — you just have to put yourself there and open up your mind, and you'll see it and feel it. Blokes like Number Nine, Old Powelly, Johnny the horse-tailer, Steve the mackerel fisherman, Ronny, the girls from Hay Street and all the other characters I've mentioned in this book — I take my hat off and salute

Phil after a few quiet beers at Daly Waters pub NT.

them, because they are the people who make us different. It's their spirit and individuality that make Australia unique in the world, and it's from their foundation that we go forward.

Although I haven't actually amounted to much myself, I still consider myself very lucky and also kind of honoured to be able to drift around as I do in this great country. It would have been good if some of my jobs had panned out a bit better, but to be quite honest, if a steady job jumped up and bit me on the arse, I don't think I'd know what to do with it. But I suppose that's just me.

I bet you're wondering what I'm doing now for a crust. Well, a few months ago I got the big idea to buy a microphone and an amplifier. I was going to rock up to pubs and sing my heart out and no doubt make a lot of money, but as usual it hasn't all gone to plan and all I've made so far is two cans of Victoria Bitter and a roast dinner.

It's starting to shape up into the 102nd adventure that got me absolutely nowhere . . .

Acknowledgements

A special thanks to my sister Marilyn, who worked very hard on this book and typed her guts out, and my brother-in-law Allan Hoffman, who also put in a lot of time and encouragement.

To my mum, who put me up and supplied a feed while I went through the rigours of writing a book, many thanks.

To my brother John, and Kylie: thanks for the thoughts from the west.

David and Christine Harris: thank you for all your advice and total optimism; it's nice to have someone to call on when the going gets tough.

Sophie Howarth: thank you for some great photos; also thank you to 'sea dog' Mark Johnson for some rippers.

Unfortunately, none of them will make any money out of this; they only helped because they're lovers of fine literature.

Design was by Christa Moffit, Christabella Design: thanks, Christa, for pulling this together.

Thanks to Geoff Morrison for your support and artistic input.

Thanks to all my mates in the Territory, all the bookshops and roadhouses and the ABC Darwin radio mob, especially Mike Prenzler.

To Jo Mackay at ABC Books for having faith in this book and for giving me a go, and also the Northern Territory Writers' Centre — it's been great, and although I'm still broke and going nowhere fast, I want to say thanks for all your help.

Finally, a sad farewell to my old mate Paul Cotton who passed away while I was putting this book together. True friends are hard to find, and Paul will be sadly missed . . . but not forgotten.